JESUS
IS
LORD

by

Susan Pryor

**"For I proclaim the name of the LORD;
Ascribe greatness to our God!"**

Deuteronomy 32:3

Jesus is Lord

Author: Susan Pryor

Interior Design: Randall Johnson

Cover Design: Brandon Johnson

ISBN: 978-1-935018-32-2

Susan Pryor

jpryoroo1@stny.rr.com

Scriptures in this book were quoted from the New American Standard Bible, the Open Edition, Thomas Nelson, Publishers unless otherwise noted.

Published by: The International Localization Network

Through: Five Stones Publishing

ILNcenter.com

Contents

Introduction to Part One

The Open Veil

The secret things belong to the LORD our God, but the things revealed belong to us and our sons forever. Deuteronomy 29:29

It usually happens when we least expect it. But that is the way of our wonderful Lord. Jesus unexpectedly comes quietly to show us more of Himself in the times of dryness, after long periods of silence.

If someone were to take a poll, it would reveal that the majority of saints who seek His face often enjoy those most glorious moments when praying is easy, answers are swift and sure, and communion with God is oh! so sweet. But just as surely, the survey would also disclose that there are seasons when the opposite is true. For people who pray, there are golden days, but dark days, too. There are days when prayer requires endurance and persistence, when answers seem nonexistent, and communication with God is a hope rather than a reality. Those are days in which prayers are sent up to the Throne Room, but no discernible response is sent back.

It is in these times, the dry and enduring times, the prayer of faith-alone times when intimate, personal communion with God is but yesterday's memory that suddenly a breeze springs up. It moves a veil. Something is seen shining just beyond our vision. We want it.

Then, if we respond to this gentle nudge of the breath of the Spirit, whether by quietly consenting to obedience or by clamorous leaping for joy because

He has broken through, God fully reveals that which He had but partially exposed.

Suddenly we can see what we could not see. Suddenly we know what we did not know. When we accept Jesus as Savior, logos becomes rhema [Greek, meaning the written Word becomes the Living Word.]. Out of the most familiar text or oft-read Scriptures, unnoticed and undiluted, wealth gleams. And God indicates there is more if we pursue Him. Precious treasure is ours if we will but unearth it and possess it.

Perhaps other readers were as fascinated in childhood as I was by stories of cowboys and horses or of trail rides and stampedes. Perhaps, too, they, like I, imaginatively spent long hours at play either chasing down bad guys with Roy Rogers or Gene Autry or riding the towns and trails of the early American West. If so, then this quandary with prayer, this search for more of God, can be likened to a 19th century gold mine that was opened and excavated until the visible quantities of ore ran out. Then, believing that there was no more gold and that the mine was of no further use or value, it was closed and abandoned by the owner.

But one day, perhaps just to revisit the scene of so much pleasure and treasure, the owner returns, enters the mine, walks along the narrow shaft and, in the dark, stumbles over an unseen rock underfoot. This throws him into a wall with such force that it causes a small dirt slide. When the dust has settled, looking with wondering, unbelieving eyes, he realizes that the accident has uncovered a hidden vein of ore, one that had been there all the time and is richer and purer than any yet seen. It is there for him to claim, explore, dig into, enjoy, possess, and even give away if he so chooses---because he already owns it.

So too with the discovery of the most precious gold of all: the revelation of Jesus Christ as found in God's Word. Often we read certain passages of Scripture, reread them, memorize them, have Bible studies concerning them, and have sermons preached about them. After a while we sometimes believe these precious Scriptures are picked clean or played out, or that all of their precious nuggets of truth have been discovered. We think it's time to move on to other areas where we can begin anew to dig and explore.

But later, circumstances may cause us to return to these same "tapped out" treasures. As we began to reinvestigate them, we find they are not as familiar as we thought they were. More in the dark than we care to admit, we grope along obscure pathways and stumble over a Rock in our path. This collision with Jesus throws us into obstacles that, once jarred, fall away to reveal heretofore hidden biblical riches. As we look with unveiled eyes, we realize He has uncovered for us, revealed to us, allowed us to see another rich facet of His character, another thread of His truth.

In the same place we thought no longer exciting or able to yield new treasures, we discover that what now appears before us is not just nuggets, not just another vein of gold, but a mother lode of revelation as to the Person and work of the Lord.

God has uncovered it and indicated it is ours to seek out, explore, claim, dig into, mine, be illuminated and inspired by, blessed with or be given away to others. We have struck it rich! It's just the beginning of the adventure.

During one of my dry and enduring times, I found that I had no more fight in me. All I could do to continue the battle that was swirling around me was to utter in faith the simple phrase, "Jesus is Lord. Jesus is Lord." In the midst of this came a glorious peace. And then I heard the Spirit of the Lord whisper, "Yes, but why is Jesus 'Lord'?"

I couldn't answer. Such is the genesis of this book.

We as Christians say this, we sing it, and we teach it. We declare it on our lapel pins and our bumper stickers. But if pressed about it, do we know why it is true? Other than parroting someone else's opinion, do we, each of us, know why Jesus is Lord? Can we explain why He is to others? And, is He Lord just in our words, or is He Lord in our hearts?

In my wandering and stumbling in the dark, I accidentally bumped into the Rock. My collision threw me into some of my carefully erected walls of self protection and self defense, and shattered them. When the dust had settled and I got my eyes off the piles of rubble at my feet, I realized God had removed personal obstacles that kept me from clearly seeing Him or more closely relating to Him. As He opened my eyes, I didn't see just nuggets meant to enrich parts of my life; I saw rich ore, a true deep vein, treasure immeasurable, meant to change my life forever.

What is the mother lode revealed? Actually, there are two interrelated topics. The first is a newer, deeper, more personal and powerful revelation of the Jesus as Lord which includes both factual, objective truth as well as a relational, subjective point of view. This is the Open Veil. Second, as kings have kingdoms over which they rule, so Jesus as Lord has Lordship, the area over which He reigns. What this is and how we respond to it is the Open Heaven.

It is my intention to show that the search for a clear understanding of the Lord is a sometimes exciting journey on an unfamiliar path as knowing leads to doing, believing leads to experiencing, accepting leads to obeying, and the objective leads to the subjective. In short, Jesus unveiled becomes Jesus revealed. Jesus revealed is Jesus, Lord.

Part of the Open Veil is the continuing journey of salvation and learning more about God and Jesus, His Son, whom we have trusted for forgiveness of our sin and for eternal life after death. The first step is to learn the names of God, which indicate His character, and the titles of our Lord, which explain His authority, as used in both the Old and New Testaments. Because some of the original manuscripts for the Bible were written in Greek, I use some Greek terminology for the names and titles of God and Jesus.

Dear Ones,

Let Jesus be revealed in a new vein. Let Him lead us deeper. If we allow this, if we determine to dig in, if we discover new treasure in Him, if we find that He is Lord and must be obeyed, we will have the strength and wisdom needed to face the dark days that are soon on us.

If we are to be awed by the Open Veil, we need to lay a foundation. To do so, we must go back into the Old Testament and learn of the Lord.

This is the gate of the LORD; the righteous will enter through it. Psalm 118:20

Chapter 1

The Old Testament LORD

Give thanks to the LORD, for He is good; for His lovingkindness is everlasting. Oh let Israel say, "His lovingkindness is everlasting." Oh let the house of Aaron say, "His lovingkindness is everlasting." Oh let those who fear the LORD say, "His lovingkindness is everlasting.' Psalm 118:1-4

According to Hebrew scholars, to allow readers to understand precisely to whom they were referring, Biblical writers were intentionally obvious and clearly differentiated the names and titles of the Almighty.

For instance, when the word God appears, written in upper and lower case, it is always referring to the One known as Elohim, the incomparable, strong, omnipotent, holy, just, righteous One. Thus, when the very first phrase of scripture states, *"In the beginning, God created…"*, it is really saying, "In the beginning Elohim, the Mighty, originated or caused to be…."--because He could.

But the name "God" is not the only reference to the Supreme Being in our Bibles. There is another word frequently used that speaks of Him. While in English we have the single word, Lord, in the Old Testament there are at least two Hebrew words for Lord. The first of these, LORD, is a personal name and the second, Lord, is more a title or a description.

Concerning the first, LORD, whenever God's name appears written in all capital letters, whether as LORD or GOD, it is a reference to the One known in Hebrew texts as Jehovah or Yahweh.

When any word is used even once in Holy Scripture, it takes on a deep dimension of importance. It was carefully chosen and just as carefully recorded for a specific reason. The name LORD is the most often used word in the Bible, appearing over five thousand times. It is therefore staggeringly important or of supreme relevance.

In ancient times, a name was the measure of the man, so to speak. It was a revelation of his character and a description, even prophetic, of his nature. It declared who he was.

For example, Jacob's name meant usurper, supplanter or deceiver, a connotation not too many people would like. What a relief and blessing it must have been to him when the Man with whom he wrestled changed his name to Israel because he had, *"striven with men and with God and had prevailed"* (Genesis 32:28). The name Naomi meant "my delight". But when she had lost husband, sons, possessions and a daughter-in-law, she herself, recognizing the change in both her circumstances and in her attitude, said *"Call me Mara, bitter…"* (Ruth 1:20).

So too the LORD'S name is a description of His being. Derived from the root word HAYAH, His name means to be, to exist or to live. It declares that the LORD is the ever existent One who was, is, and ever will be. His character is eternal. His nature is to be alive—and to reproduce the essence of that life in us.

Knowing the number of times it appears or the importance of His name is not the only way to learn about the LORD. To gain even more understanding, **the law of first use** must be employed. The law of first use is a guideline of scripture that states that the first time a name or a title is used, that is the foundational introduction of that name or title. Its premier appearance is to cause readers to stop, examine it in context with surrounding scripture, ask questions, and determine why it is there. From its original use and placement comes the basic meaning and truth of the word. All further study of the word takes off from this initial point of contact.

Just so with the name of the LORD. In the very first chapter of the book of Genesis, we see God or Elohim in action. Busily He created and then rested. But in the second chapter of Genesis, something different is noted.

This is the account of the heavens and the earth when they were created, in the day that the LORD God made earth and heaven. Genesis 2:4

A new name or nature or description of God shines forth. In the Biblical account of creation, new information is disclosed about the Creator. He is no longer only God, but Jehovah God. He is no longer simply powerful, but alive and eternally powerful.

Even in these earliest of times, God wanted to manifest more of Himself. He was declaring that there was more to Him than had previously been revealed. He wasn't just Mighty God who could do as He wished; there was a softer side to His nature, too. He was introducing Jehovah, the eternally existing One, the self sustaining One, the non-created Being with God who was God, the LORD of life. As the wellspring or source of all life, He was there to create all forms of life: heavenly, earthly, plant, animal, and human.

Therefore, He was not just the Creator of life; He was the maintainer and sustainer of life, too. From this initial point, the name of the LORD God appears more and more often in scripture. It was the LORD God who placed Adam in the garden and gave him dominion over it. When sin entered paradise, it was the LORD God who approached Adam and Eve, the LORD God who judged them and the serpent, and the LORD God who made tunics to cover the couple. And surely in sorrow, it was the LORD God who, rather than see them entombed forever in the death of sin if they should eat of the tree of life, sent them out of the garden (Genesis 2:15; 3:14-19, 21-24).

Shortly after this, the Bible records that men began to call on the name of the LORD (Genesis 4:26).

Even as the history of man unfolded in its now more difficult way, the LORD took an active, loving part in it all. In the course of time, a special people was chosen. A special race was set aside for God alone. When that nation found itself in deep trouble, the LORD used the crisis to personally introduce Himself to those He had given life and reserved for Himself alone. It's a familiar story to the saints, the believers.

God, the all powerful but seemingly remote, spoke to a man named Abram. He promised to make him a great nation and that through him all the nations of the earth would be blessed (Genesis 12:1-3). So sure was God's announcement that He made a covenant with Abram, sealing His commitment eternally.

Faithfully, God renewed this pact with Abram's son Isaac and Isaac's son, Jacob. Jacob, grandson of Abram, had twelve sons. One of these, Joseph, appeared lost to him. Years later famine tried to devour the rest. In desperation, Jacob sent some of his sons to Egypt to buy grain and there, they discovered their "lost" brother, second in command only to Pharaoh. At Joseph's urging, they and their whole families moved to Egypt.

Thus began a sojourn of the people which lasted over four hundred years. When the Israelites first arrived in Egypt, because they were near kin of the second most powerful man in the empire, they were highly favored and given the best of the land. Years later, when the king of Egypt died, they fell into dishonor and then bondage. Beaten, whipped, tortured, killed, they were slaves to the mere whims of Pharaoh.

Wisely they cried out. Not to the gods of the people or land around them, but rather to the Elohim of their ancestors, they sent up their pleas (Exodus

2:23). Mercifully, He responded. He heard their groanings and remembered His covenant with their forefathers. He looked on them and acknowledged them (Exodus 2:24,25).

As the Angel of the LORD, the eternal, loving, living Sovereign, He appeared in a fiery flame to a man called Moses. Declaring that He was the God of Abraham, Isaac, and Jacob, He commissioned Moses to be His representative or human deliverer.

And now, behold, the cry of the sons of Israel has come to Me; furthermore, I have seen the oppression with which the Egyptians are oppressing them. Therefore, come now, and I will send you to Pharaoh, so that you may bring My people, the sons of Israel, out of Egypt. Exodus 3:9,10

And Moses, just as many of us would have done, balked. His first question to God was, *"Who am I...?"* (verse 11).

In response, God made two promises: first, His presence would go with Moses and second, when Moses succeeded in bringing God's people to freedom, they would all return to worship Him on that very mountain (verse 12).

In other words, no matter how dangerous, no matter how fearful or traumatic the days ahead would be, he and God's people would live through it. Success was guaranteed. Powerful God could make it happen.

Yet, even as gracious, glorious and reassuring as that may have been, Moses wasn't yet satisfied. Bravely he pressed on, trying to identify who was speaking to him and who was about to change the course of history. Though he now knew what God intended to do, he wanted to learn more about who He was. He wanted to know by whose authority he was to act. He wanted a personal ID as it were.

As Moses pressed in, as he drew closer to God, an interesting change occurred. Suddenly his question shifted. Instead of continuing to question, *"Who am I?"*, he now widened his area of interest and asked in effect, "Who are You?" (verse 13). Rather than demanding a testimony of what God could do, he asked to understand His nature. In essence, he asked for a character reference. He wanted God to declare who He was by revealing His name.

And God answered! Mercifully condescending to explain Himself to man, He did exactly as He had been asked to do. He revealed His name.

> *Then Moses said to God, "Behold, I am going to the sons of Israel, and I shall say to them, 'The God of your fathers has sent me to you.' Now they may say to me, 'What is His name?' What shall I say to them?" And God said to Moses, I AM WHO I AM; and He said, "Thus you shall say to the sons of Israel, 'I AM has sent me to you.'" Exodus 3:13,14*

Since the name given is written in all capital letters, I AM WHO I AM, it is the LORD. He is Jehovah, the author of life. And in entering the fray to free the Hebrews from the scourge of slavery in Egypt, He was about to prove He could sustain life, too. Since the one thing those many captive, tortured souls in Egypt needed was life, they had obviously connected with the right name. The LORD was about to enter their death scene to bring life.

But the LORD is not the only holy One to make Himself known to ancient Israel. This people was also blessed to know the Lord.

Ascribe to the LORD, O families of the peoples, ascribe to the LORD glory and strength. Ascribe to the LORD the glory of His name; bring an offering, and come into His courts. Worship the LORD in holy attire; tremble before Him, all the earth. Say among the nations, "The LORD reigns;" (Psalm 96:7-10)

Chapter 2

The Old Testament Lord

I will give thanks to Thee, O Lord my God, with all my heart and will glorify Thy name forever. Psalm 86:12

If now we are more familiar with and comfortable about our relationship with the LORD, it is time to press on.

In our study so far, we know that differentiating the names of God would be as follows:

1. God - written with upper and lower case letters is Elohim, the One known to the patriarchs and whose primary attribute is strength.

2. LORD or GOD - depicted with all letters capitalized is Jehovah, the personal name of God, and the One who was--and is--the self existent, eternal, unchanging Author of life.

But two words are not sufficient to define or describe our great God. When reading the Bible, there is the third name or title that constantly and enthusiastically appears. This is the Lord.

3. Lord - written with a capital and lower case letters is Adonay or Adonai.

Before delving into a more complete study, a quick contrast of the LORD and the Lord is helpful. First, in the Bible, Jehovah is a name, while Adonai is more a statement of position or a title of respect. Second, the name LORD or Jehovah always and only refers to the supreme One, God.

As studying the derivation of the name LORD gave much information as to His character, nature, and being, so learning of the title Lord yields rich nuggets of truth.

Concerning the human level, the word "lord" has two primary meanings. One of these involves ownership; a lord is one who has or possesses. The other involves authority; a lord is leader or ruler. He is head or chief of others, one with power over them. He is, in his own defined realm, a sovereign, one with the right to rule. He is master of his own domain. The idea here is that of lord-vassal, master-servant, superior-underling relationship. Thus, one who owns, rules. Because he possesses, he leads. He occupies the position of headship or exercises his authority over those people and possessions that belong to him.

According to the law of first use, Abram was the first man called lord. His wife, Sarah, speaks of him.

> *And Sarah laughed to herself, saying, "After I have become old, shall I have pleasure, my lord being old also?" Genesis 18:12*

Sara refers-or defers-to her husband, Abram. In calling him lord, she is proclaiming his headship; she announces or acknowledges his authority over her. In essence, she states his position as head of the household and submits to his position as such. Though she is struggling with doubt about the prophetic word concerning him, she is in no way denying or rejecting his rule over her. The testimony in the New Testament scripture confirms her intent.

> *It was thus that Sarah obeyed Abraham "following his guidance and acknowledging his headship over her by calling him lord (master, leader, authority) 1 Peter 3:6; AMP*

After Sarah introduced the use of the term lord, others followed her lead. In later ages and times, to other people, lord was a courtesy title or a mark of deference to one in authority. For example, Jacob, returning home from a twenty-year sojourn in Paddam-aram, once again faced his older brother who had wanted to murder him. He addressed Esau as, "*My lord!* (Genesis 33: 8,13). Joseph declared himself to be lord of pharaoh's house, "*a ruler throughout all the land of Egypt*" (Genesis 45:8). Joshua called Moses lord (Numbers 11:28) and Ruth so honored Boaz (Ruth 2:13). David, even when Saul's treachery had sent him fleeing, yet honored Saul as lord (1 Samuel 26:17) and Daniel, in the face of possible death, called Nebuchadnezzar lord (Daniel 4:19).

But the title lord is not confined to the human realm. Even more awesome is its divine significance. In fact, the most brilliant human leadership or most powerful exercise of authority is but a shadow of the holy. It dims in comparison with that of the true Lord, Adonai.

In scripture, Adonai is very special. He is **the** Lord. The **only** One. The **true** One. In His relationship with men, He fills both roles that human lords do. First, He is Owner and Possessor **of** all He created; and second, He is Master and Ruler **over** all He created. He is Head of His chosen people. He is the only One with all authority and power.

Though human lords have measured land areas and certain possessions, there is no limitation to the possessions of Adonai. He is Lord all of the earth (Joshua 3:11).

Similarly, the rule of human lords is confined to definite (whether large or small) parameters. They rule or have mastery over what they own but can not extend their authority over anyone else's household, possessions, or domain. But the divine Lord has no such restrictions. His rule is in no way and in no area limited. He is Head over all men who have, do now, or ever will exist. He is Leader of saved and unsaved alike. He is Chief over the multitudes of families, tribes, races and nations. He is even Lord of all human rulers who wield authority and power: He is Lord of kings (Daniel 2:47) and Lord of lords (Deuteronomy 10:17).

The title Adonai even denotes the character of this most powerful Leader or Lord. It speaks of His beauty (Psalm 90:17), majesty, glory, and power. It declares His uniqueness (Exodus 8:10); He is the One with absolute dominion over all creation. Because this Lord is good (Jeremiah 3:12) and this Lord is great (Nehemiah 4:14), because He is righteous (Daniel 9:14) and holy (Psalm 99:9), those ruled over never had to worry that His immense, immeasurable authority would be used in the wrong way or against those He so dearly loved.

While Sarah, speaking of Abram, was the first to use the human title, lord, to honor her husband, Abram, it was that same Abram who in turn was the first to use the divine name, Lord. After being promised by the LORD of life that he would have a son and eventually be the father of a multitude (Genesis 13:16), Abram was concerned that he remained childless. If he died without issue or heir, all his possessions would go to his servant, Eliezer. He offered a prayer, not to the LORD, but to the Lord GOD--to Adonai Jehovah.

> *And Abram said, "O Lord GOD, what wilt Thou give me, since I am childless, and the heir of my house is Eliezer of Damascus?" Genesis 15:2*

And when reassured that life, a son from his own body, would be forthcoming (Genesis 15:4), he again petitioned the Lord GOD concerning the land that had been promised.

> *And he said," O Lord GOD, how may I know that I shall possess it? Genesis 15:8*

Why did he do this? The first petition dealt with a life issue. The Lord GOD, Jehovah, was the source and producer of the life promised. The second prayer dealt with ownership. Since he had been promised land, it was the Lord, Adonai, the Owner and Possessor of all land who had authority to release Abram's portion to him. It was only He who had the sovereignty and power to bring these things to pass.

What can be said of this wonderful Old Testament Adonai? Not nearly enough! A thousand tongues could not altogether through all eternity fully declare Him or honor Him. As foundationally as it can be expressed, the Lord is the supreme, supernatural, holy, spiritual authority. He is Sovereign God.

But Thou, O Lord, art a God merciful and gracious, slow to anger and abundant and loving-kindness and truth. Psalm 86:15

ॐ

Chapter 3

Who are
Jehovah and Adonai?

Jesus answered, "HEAR, O ISRAEL! THE LORD OUR GOD IS ONE LORD; Mark 12:29

It is highly significant that Abram's pleas in Genesis 15:2 and 8 included both the title Lord and the name LORD. The former was used to petition Jehovah to create life; the latter was to ask Adonai to exercise His rightful authority or to extend His power on Abrams' behalf. Functioning together, or as One, Abram knew the work would be done, the promise fulfilled.

To some, this double petition of name and title may cause a problem or raise a question? Are Jehovah and Adonai two separate holy Ones?

The answer is an emphatic NO! There are not two Lords but one. The LORD Jehovah and the Lord Adonai are One.

It is scripture that brings credence to that statement. Psalm 8:1 succinctly begins:

O LORD, our Lord…

In four short words, there is profound truth. First, the LORD is the Lord. There is no contradiction, no competition, no duality. The Creator of life is also the Ruler over life. While the name tells who He is and the title announces what He does, both describe one Being. Jehovah is Adonai.

Also, the use of the third word in the above scripture, our, brings in the element of possession. Surely the Jehovah who creates must be acknowledged as the Adonai who owns and rules. And just as surely, since He created us and gave us eternal life through faith in Him, He owns and rules us. We are His.

But His ownership of us is not what this scripture is emphasizing. The intent of these words is not to disclose His possession of us but ours of Him. Jehovah is our LORD. Adonai is our Lord. While we are His, He is ours! That is, in every holy, reverent sense, we possess, hold, have the Possessor.

How ironic and how awesome!

A second question along this same line might arise. If we factor the name of God in with those of the LORD and the Lord, are there three supreme Beings? Again, the answer is a quick and definite NO!

As we accept by faith that there is a Trinity or one God in three Persons, Father, Son, and Holy Spirit, so also we can acknowledge that there is one God who needs many names, descriptions, and titles to define His Being and to reveal His supremacy. Because this one God is so beyond the ability of the human mind to imagine, analyze, or fully know, multiple portraits of His Person are required. Each of these descriptive revelations discloses His multi-faceted Being just in part so that, by His blessing and grace, when put together, they unite to bring fuller understanding of the whole.

Two such expressions of God are LORD and Lord. In truth, the only omniscient, omnipresent, omnipotent God is both Jehovah and Adonai.

Again, it is scripture that bears witness to this sweeping statement. Deuteronomy 4:35 once announced to Israel and now declares to the church that Jehovah is God. "*To you it was shown that you might know that the LORD is God; there is no other besides Him"* (see also Psalm 100:3). The Word also clearly states that the Lord is God. *"For...God is...Lord of lords"*. In fact, nothing could be more emphatic than the full statement of Deuteronomy 10:17 that links all three names in question.

For the LORD your God is the God of gods and the Lord of lords, the great, the mighty, and the awesome God who does not show partiality, nor take a bribe.

Thus there are not two Lords or three supreme Beings. There is but One. The LORD is God---who also is the Lord.

"AND YOU SHALL LOVE THE LORD YOUR GOD WITH ALL YOUR HEART, AND WITH ALL YOUR SOUL, AND WITH ALL YOUR MIND, AND WITH ALL YOUR STRENGTH." Mark 12:30

ॐ

Chapter 4

Isaiah's Open Veil

In the year of King Uzziah's death, I saw the Lord sitting on a throne, lofty and exalted with the train of His robe filling the temple. Isaiah 6:1

Now that we have a foundational understanding that the LORD, the eternal Being who produces and sustains life is also the Lord, the sovereign Ruler over all, portions of the Old Testament become much more exciting.

In these early scriptures, in the Hebrew Pentateuch and Law, in Psalms and Proverbs, in the books of Kings and Prophets, there is talk of such a LORD as this dwelling on earth. There is more than just the hint of the personal presence of the Holy One coming to live among men, a LORD who could be seen, who could be heard, and whose presence could be visibly, physically felt.

One of the prophets is especially instrumental in revealing this coming. Throughout the book of Isaiah, there are multitudes of references to this beloved LORD. For instance, it is Isaiah who succinctly declared the birth of the coming One.

"For a child will be born to us, a son will be given to us; and the government will rest on His shoulders; and His name will be called Wonderful Counselor, Mighty God, Eternal Father, Prince of Peace." Isaiah 9:6

Such a blessing is described as the work of the LORD.

> *There will be no end to the increase of His government or of peace,*
> *on the throne of David and over his kingdom, to establish it*
> *and to uphold it with justice and righteousness from then on and*
> *forevermore.* **The zeal of the LORD of hosts will accomplish**
> **this**. *Isaiah 9:7 (emphasis mine)*

Quickly following that prophecy is a detailed description of the Spirit of this LORD.

> *And the Spirit of the LORD will rest on Him, the spirit of wisdom and*
> *understanding, the spirit of counsel and strength, the spirit of knowl-*
> *edge and the fear of the LORD. Isaiah 11:2*

Further, the whole of chapter 25 is a song of praise, an exaltation of the LORD as Deliverer. And after chapter upon chapter dealing with rebuke, warning and judgment, suddenly Isaiah speaks of comfort to the people of God by again foretelling the coming of this LORD, the One of extraordinary birth and with extraordinary Spirit (Isaiah 40:3). Isaiah then goes on to announce that the LORD will declare new things (Isaiah 42:9). Surely, Isaiah 53 is one of the best known passages of scripture. Detailing the blessing of atonement, it is well worth a review for its insistent references to the goodness of the LORD in dealing with our sin.

How could Isaiah speak forth such compelling and prophetically proven words? Why was his relationship and understanding of the LORD so intimate?

Perhaps the impetus of his revelations of the compassionate, merciful side of the LORD comes from the derivation of his own name. Isaiah means salvation is of the Lord. Or, perhaps it came because the fear and the reverence of the Lord fell on him very early in his sixty or so years as a prophet and, from that awesome moment on, never left him.

What was this momentous, life changing event that threw him into the arms of the LORD? In the eighth century BC, Judah seemed ready to follow its neighbor Israel into ungodliness, faithlessness, decline, and apostasy. Even as the nation and people were turning away from their covenant and their LORD, God raised up and sent Isaiah onto the scene to be His voice to the people. Even from the first verses of his message, he plunged into the problems before him and wasted no time exposing the truth. His words rang out to declare the evil of the day.

> *The vision of Isaiah the son of Amoz, concerning Judah and Jerusalem which he saw during the reigns of Uzziah, Jotham, Ahaz, and Hezekiah, kings of Judah. Listen, O heavens, and hear, O earth; for the LORD speaks, "Sons I have reared and brought up, but they have revolted against Me. Isaiah 1:1,2*

As he proceeded to reveal the extent of the problem involving so many people, his words were harsh.

> *For behold, the Lord GOD (or, the Master who is mighty upon you) of hosts is going to remove from Jerusalem and Judah both supply and support, the whole supply of bread, and the whole supply of water; the mighty man and the warrior, the judge and the prophet, the diviner and the elder, the captain of fifty and the honorable man, the counselor and the expert artisan, and the skillful enchanter. And I will make mere lads their princes and capricious children will rule over them and the people will be oppressed... Isaiah 3:1-5*

> *Moreover, the LORD said, "Because the daughters of Zion are proud, and walk with heads held high and seductive eyes, and go along with mincing steps and tinkle the bangles on their feet, therefore the Lord will afflict the scalp of the daughters of Zion with scabs, and the LORD will make their foreheads bare" (verses16,17).*

Your men will fall by the sword, and your mighty ones in battle, And her gates will lament and mourn; and deserted she will sit on the ground (verses 25,26).

Finally, after another lengthy passage, he promises judgment.

Therefore as a tongue of fire consumes stubble, and dry grass collapses into the flame, so their root will become like rot and their blossom blow away as dust; for they have rejected the law of the LORD of hosts, and despised the word of the Holy One of Israel. On this account the anger of the LORD has burned against His people, and He has stretched out His hand against them and struck them down, and the mountains quaked; and their corpses lay like refuse in the middle of the streets. For all this His anger is not spent, but His hand is still stretched out. He will also lift up a standard to the distant nation, and will whistle for it from the ends of the earth; and behold, it will come with speed swiftly. No one in it is weary or stumbles, none slumbers or sleeps; nor is the belt at its waist undone, nor its sandal strap broken. Its arrows are sharp, and all its bows are bent; the hoofs of its horses seem like flint, and its chariot wheels like a whirlwind. Its roaring is like a lioness, and it roars like young lions; it growls as it seizes the prey, and carries it off with no one to deliver it. And it shall growl over it in that day like the roaring of the sea. If one looks to the land, behold, there is darkness and distress; even the light is darkened by its clouds. Isaiah 5:24-30

Yet, in the midst of what can best be described as a horror scene, against this backdrop of impending doom and disaster, Isaiah saw it. God drew back the veil separating natural from supernatural, human from holy. He gave Isaiah supernatural sight so that he could see what was usually unseen. And Isaiah saw the Open Veil. He saw through the Open Veil. His own words best describe the experience.

In the year of King Uzziah's death, I saw the Lord sitting on a throne, lofty and exalted, with the train of His robe filling the temple. Sera-

phim stood above Him, each having six wings; with two he covered his
face, and with two he covered his feet, and two he flew. And one called
out to another and said, "Holy, Holy, Holy, is the LORD of hosts, the
whole earth is full of His glory." And the foundations of the thresholds
trembled at the voice of him who called out, while the temple was fill-
ing with smoke. Isaiah 6:1-4

Isaiah saw the Lord. He saw sovereign God, ruler of all men, Lord of heaven
and earth, Leader of kings and lords. He saw his Lord sitting on a throne,
the posture and place of authority, with His train filling His temple.

Furthermore, Isaiah's ears were opened to hear supernatural sounds. He
heard the seraphim honoring, worshipping, and declaring the glories of the
LORD Almighty, the eternal God. Such was the power and majesty and
glory of the sound that the thresholds trembled.

Just as wondrous as the sight and sound of God in heaven is Isaiah's reaction
to them. His first response was death. Death to self. All he could say when
immersed in the glories of the Lord was, *"Woe is me, for I am ruined."* Other
versions of the Bible translate these words as, *"I am undone!* (NKJV) or, *"I*
am undone and ruined" (AMP). All of these can well be summarized by
the words of the Jerusalem Bible, *"What a retched state I am in! I am*
lost…". (Isaiah 6:5)

We can only guess the horror in Isaiah when, in touching heaven, the com-
parisons of his humanity with the Lord's holiness and his earthiness with
heaven's awesomeness became apparent to him.

In this Open Veil event, God made no word of rebuke; in fact, He was honoring Isaiah with a supernatural experience. But Isaiah's own standards, his
own value system instantly recognized the immeasurable distance between
himself and the Lord who he saw and the heavenly voices that he heard, and
he was undone.

Furthermore, since Isaiah's calling was as prophet, he was to be a mouth-
piece, a messenger of God to the people. In a flash of insight, as the sights

and sounds of heaven surrounded and overwhelmed him, he realized that what should have been a strength, his voice, was in reality a weakness. He understood he was ruined and undone specifically," *because I am a man of unclean lips, and I live among a people of unclean lips.*" (Isaiah 6:5).

But a second reaction to this miraculous presentation of eternity is recorded, too. It is life.

The instant Isaiah made his confession of sin, a seraph sprang into action, bringing healing and forgiveness to Isaiah.

> *"Then one of the seraphim flew to me, having in his hand a live coal which he had taken with the tongs from the altar. And he touched my mouth with it, and said: "Behold, this has touched your lips; your iniquity is taken away, and your sin purged."* Isaiah 6:6,7

And when this prophet was made presentable, it was the Lord, the One Isaiah had seen, who asked, "*Whom shall I send, and who will go for Us?*" (verse 8). Such awe, such dread, such amazement, such astonishment, such worship filled Isaiah that he cried out, "*Here I am! Send me.*" (verse 8). He committed himself to life in the service of the very Lord who had engulfed him and who had exchanged his human voice for a higher calling.

Perhaps because he saw through the Open Veil, perhaps because he saw the Lord and got a firsthand glimpse of the courts of heaven, and surely because he had been prepared, healed, and forgiven, Isaiah could go on to keep his commitment of service and obedience. His recorded words, referred to earlier, are some of the most scathing and portentous as well as some of the most sublime and delightful in all of Scripture. When he saw the Lord, he could speak of the Lord. When he spoke of the Lord, others could see the Lord. Thank You, Lord, for opening his eyes. Thank You for his Open Veil.

For whenever a man turns to the Lord, the veil is taken away. 2 Corinthians 3:16

Chapter 5

The New Testament Lord

For there is no distinction between Jew and Greek; for the same Lord is Lord of all, abounding in riches for all who call upon Him… Romans 10:12

But such blessing, such awe, such knowledge and vision of the glory of the Lord is not confined to the Old Testament alone. In the New Testament, Father God blesses His people in some unusual and delightful ways, too. One of these is the gift of the revelation of the New Testament Lord.

From our study of the Old Testament, we know that both words for Lord, whether the LORD, the eternal, self-existent, unchanging Creator of life, or the Lord, the Master Ruler or Sovereign, refer to one divine Being. But neither of them, except in reference to Old Testament scripture or prophecy, appears as such in the New Testament. In New Covenant scripture, the word for Lord is the Greek word, Kurios.

And so, more questions arise! What is a kurios? Who is the Kurios? What is His name? In other words, even though we know who was LORD and Lord of Old Testament people and times, do we know who is Lord of the New? Is this Lord the same one that Isaiah and others said was coming, or is He someone else? Is He the same Lord that Isaiah saw or is He One that is new and different?

According to <u>Vine's Expository Dictionary of Biblical Words</u>, a kurios is one having power and authority. When kurios is written lower case in New Testament scripture in reference to **a** man, this title means a lord, one with authority to govern and the right to rule (Mark 10:42). It also means a master, one whom slaves must obey. Too, a human kurios was an owner of particular goods and possessions. Finally, he was commonly addressed as sir, a title of respect used when speaking to or about one in authority (such as father or husband).

But when Kurios is written in scripture in reference to **the** Man, its meaning transcends all human importance and significance. It reflects the divine. The capitalized Kurios indicated that there is an identity to discover beyond that of mere man and his circumstances. This Kurios is Ruler. He is not in authority over one particular domain, but Sovereign over all things. When He declared, for instance, that, *"the Son of Man is Lord of the Sabbath,"* (Matthew 12:8), He meant that He had the right to declare the way that He, not man, wished the Sabbath to be celebrated.

This Kurios is Master. Since no man can honorably or righteously serve two masters (Matthew 6:24), He is the one Master all must choose to submit to, the One all must decide to obey. This Kurios is Owner of all things. And this Kurios is Sir, always due the full respect of those speaking to or about him, the One who must forever be given honor where honor is due.

In the seventh chapter of Matthew's gospel, in exposing false leaders, in judging their fruit, and warning that their expectation of reward for carnal, self-declared works might be futile, this Lord spoke out very strongly.

"Not everyone who says to Me, 'Lord, Lord,' will enter the kingdom of heaven; but he who does the will of My Father who is in heaven. Many will say to Me on that day, 'Lord, Lord, did we not prophesy in Your name, and in Your name cast out demons, and in Your name

perform many miracles?' And I will declare to them, 'I never knew you'" Matthew 7:21-23

His choice of the word for Leader or Sovereign was carefully chosen. He was specifically and clearly revealing that this name and title were His alone. In stating that, "many will say **to Me**", He was not denying the title of Lord but purposefully assuming it. He was publicly declaring, "I am Lord." Further, His double use of the word, that is, His saying, "Lord, Lord" makes His pronouncement even more emphatic.

While twentieth century Christians have the benefit of millennia of hindsight and history, first century disciples did not. When this Lord appeared on the scene, He presented two problems. First, people saw Him as a mere man, the son of Joseph and Mary, who seemed to be assigning to Himself divine status. This was an affront to their social and cultural traditions. Second, Pharisees and elders saw Him as a human being who was being hailed as King, Prophet, and Messiah. This was an offense to their religious beliefs and status.

During His short years of active, public ministry, some people (Matthew 8:2) and disciples (Matthew 8:25) who accepted His revealed identity did address Him as Lord. Yet, as other people and religious leaders struggled to make adjustments in their evaluation of this Man and respond to this lord as the Lord, He became subject to a deep rooted hysteria in His challenge to tradition. People solved the dilemma of identification by killing the human man. But they could not kill the divine Lord.

In rising from the dead, He was quickly given the title and status of Lord. As Vine's says of Him, "His purpose did not become clear to the disciples until after His resurrection, and the revelation of His Deity consequent thereon. Thomas, when he realized the significance of the presence of a mortal wound in the body of a living man, immediately joined with it the absolute title of Deity, saying, 'My Lord and my God' (John 20:28). Thereafter, except in Acts 10:4 and Revelation 7:14, there is no record that kurios was ever again used by believers in addressing any save God and the Lord Jesus…" (pg. 379).

These truths are authenticated in the Word. God honored this Lord's sacrifice unto death by raising Him to life and exalting Him to the highest place. He made Him Lord so that each of us can have the privilege of bowing before Him to worship Him and submit to His authority.

The New Testament Kurios is no stranger to us. He is Lord of all (Acts 10:36). He is the Lord sinners must believe in and call upon to be saved (Acts 16:31). He is the Lord to whom saints must cry out for help (Matthew 8:25).

His name is Jesus.

And being found in appearance as a man, He humbled Himself by becoming obedient to the point of death, even death on a cross. Therefore also God highly exalted Him, and bestowed on Him the name which is above every name, that at the name of Jesus, every knee should bow, of those who are in heaven, and on earth, and under the earth, and that every tongue should confess that Jesus Christ is Lord, to the glory of God the Father. Phillipians. 2:8-11

Chapter 6

Jesus is LORD

O come, let us sing for joy to the LORD; let us shout joyfully to the rock of our salvation. Let us come before His presence with thanksgiving; let us shout joyfully to Him with psalms. For the LORD is a great God, and a great King above all gods... Psalm 95: 1-3

Surely some of the questions raised in the last chapter have been answered. For instance, we know that a kurios is a lord and that the Kurios is Lord. And it is He, Jesus, who is Kurios of New Testament times and people.

Now, we must seek information on the final two queries: 1) Is He the One that Isaiah and others said would come, or is He someone else altogether? 2) Is this New Testament Lord the same as the Old Testament LORD and Lord, or is He One who is new and different?

After many prophetic warnings of disaster if His people did not return to God, the Old Testament ends badly. For so long so many had spoken! For long so many had heard! For so long so many had ignored! And then came silence. Those who would not hear could not hear. Years and years of silence went by. Dead silence. Whole generations and centuries passed without the voice of God being heard.

If any have prayed, persisted, pressed in, endured and yet heard nothing from God, they can identify with silence. If any have gone through years in the wilderness, they know about the isolation of lack of communication. If any have suffered through the dark night of the soul, they know the desolation of the Lord removing His discernible presence. Darkness and silence kill.

Such was the condition of the Israelites when suddenly, after four hundred years of such silence, a sound is heard; a cry goes forth. From the depths of barrenness, out of the bleakness of the dry desert—a physical place as well as a spiritual condition—a voice is heard. Publicly, prophetically, the voice rang out.

Does it strike any of us how incredibly merciful that first message was? It was not a redeclaration of the Ten Commandments with a forceful exhortation to do better in keeping them! It was not a list of miscreants who God was going to lay low because of their sin! It was not the thunderous taunting of what might have been if the chosen ones had chosen to obey Him! It was rather a glorious word, a forgiving word, a hope producing word spoken by one called John the Baptist. Quoting almost exactly the words of the prophet Isaiah (Isaiah 40:3-5), his message too proclaimed the coming of the LORD who is both God and Lord.

> "THE VOICE OF ONE CRYING IN THE WILDERNESS. 'MAKE READY THE WAY OF THE LORD. MAKE HIS PATHS STRAIGHT. EVERY RAVINE SHALL BE FILLED UP, AND EVERY MOUNTAIN AND HILL SHALL BE BROUGHT LOW; AND THE CROOKED SHALL BECOME STRAIGHT, AND THE ROUGH ROADS SMOOTH; AND ALL FLESH SHALL SEE THE SALVATION OF GOD.'" Luke 3:4-6
>
> (Note: The New American Standard Bible Old Testament Scripture quoted in the New Testament is written in caps.)

Who was this LORD? By preparing the way of the LORD, John was preparing the way of Jesus. He was therefore forcefully and purposefully announcing that Jesus was the LORD. He was in fact declaring that his relative (Luke 1:36), Jesus, was Jehovah.

Was John right? Had he correctly understood his calling? Was he speaking truth? Was Jesus the long awaited LORD?

The agreement of two or three witnesses is readily available through scripture. First, the statement that Jesus is LORD is corroborated by the apostle Peter. His words, *"if you have tasted the kindness of the LORD,"* (1 Peter 2:3) are a direct reference to the Old Testament passage, *"O taste and see that the LORD is good,"* (Psalm 34:8). If carefully studied, it becomes obvious that Peter is speaking of Jesus and the psalmist of Yahweh. Therefore, Jesus and Yahweh or Jehovah are One.

Paul is another New Testament giant who confirms the astonishing identity of the LORD. He was familiar with the words of the Old Testament prophet Joel who said:

> *And it will come about that whoever calls on the name of the LORD will be delivered; for on Mount Zion and in Jerusalem there will be those who escape, as the LORD has said, even among the survivors whom the LORD calls. Joel 2:32*

Though Joel was referring to the LORD, when Paul quoted the well known phrase, *"whoever will call upon the name of the LORD will be saved"* (Romans 10:13), he was referring to Jesus (see verse 9). To him, too, the LORD and Jesus were the same Being.

But who is the best witness of all? Who knew even better than John the Baptist, Peter or Paul who the LORD was? Another witness testifies whose word is irrefutable. It is the very One whose name is in question: Jesus. In specific reference to the Old Testament name of the LORD or I AM WHO I AM, Jesus revealed the truth of His identity.

Of great significance is an encounter He had with some Pharisees who questioned His parentage (John 8:19) and His identity (verse 25). After proudly boasting over their own heritage, *"Abram is our father"* (verse 39) and denouncing Him as a demon possessed Samaritan (verse 48), Jesus could not have been more explosively direct or emphatically confrontational when He revealed His own ancestry.

> *Jesus said to them, "Most assuredly, I say to you, before Abraham was born, I AM." John 8:58; NKJV*

Remembering the Old Testament code for the names of God, since His words I AM are written with all capital letters and He was describing Himself by them, Jesus was announcing that He was the LORD.

In a similar encounter with Sadducees who wanted to promote their own erroneous religious beliefs, He declared, "I am the God of Abraham, and the God of Isaac and the god of Jacob." (Matthew 22:32). In essence Jesus was revealing, "I am I AM." Or, "I am the LORD, Jehovah."

Throughout much of the book of John, He repeated His words in order to add to the list of His names and further reveal His Being.

- *I am the bread of life.*---John 6:35

- *I am the light of the world.*---John 8:12

- *I am the door.* ---John 10:9

- *I am the good shepherd.*---John 10:14

- *I am the resurrection and the life.*---John 11:25

- *I am the way, the truth and the life.*---John 14:6

- *I am He.*---John 18:6

Without any doubt, by prophecy and by revelation, Jesus is the Old Testament LORD.

In other ways than the revelation of His name, the word confirms that Jesus is LORD. As Jehovah is eternal, so Jesus *"ever lives"* (Hebrews 7:25). As Jehovah is unchanging, so Jesus *"is the same yesterday, today and forever"* (Hebrews 13:8). The Old Testament reveals the LORD as Creator; and the New Testament, referring to Jesus, says He, *"in the beginning did lay the foundation of the earth and the heavens are the works of His hands"* (Hebrews 1:10). Jehovah created life; Jesus came, not only that we might have life but that we might have it abundantly (John 10:10). Jehovah is the Maintainer and Sustainer of life; Jesus is the One who gave His life that we might live.

There can be no doubt that just as the Old Testament LORD is Jesus, so the New Testament Kurios is Jesus. Can we then begin to understand the importance of the words used by those who once cried out to Jesus? Can we join the growing chorus of those who are crying out to Him today?

> Blessed is He who came.
> Blessed is He who comes again.
> Blessed is He who comes in the name of the LORD (Matt. 21:9)
> His name is Jesus.
> Come, Lord Jesus!
> ...the Spirit and the bride say, "Come!" (Rev. 22:17)

Come, let us worship and bow down; let us kneel before the LORD our Maker. For He is our God, and we are the people of His pasture and sheep of His hand. Psalm 95:6,7

Chapter 7

Jesus is Lord

For this reason I too, having heard of the faith in the Lord Jesus which exists among you, and your love for all the saints, do not cease giving thanks for you while making mention of you in my prayers; that the God of our Lord Jesus Christ , the Father of glory, may give to you a spirit of wisdom and of revelation in the knowledge of Him. I pray that the eyes of your heart may be enlightened, so that you may know what is the hope of His calling, what are the riches of the glory of His inheritance in the saints, and what is the surpassing greatness of His power toward us who believe. These are in accordance with the working of the strength of His might which He brought about in Christ, when He raised Him from the dead, and seated Him at His right hand in the heavenly places, far above all rule and authority and power and dominion, and every name that is named, not only in this age, but also in the one to come. Ephesians 1:15-21

We have come to the heart of the message. We have arrived at the very crux of the matter. As Jesus, the New Testament Kurios is LORD, so also Jesus, the New Testament Kurios, is Lord. The basis of our faith, that which solemnly yet joyfully sets Christianity apart from all other worldwide religions and cults and that which sanctifies and separates it from all other idols and gods is the tenet that to the glory of God the Father, Jesus Christ is Lord.

Surely from the time each of us received the gift of salvation by grace through faith in the Person and name of Jesus Christ, we have **heard** that Jesus is Lord. It is also highly likely that from the time of our first reborn baby steps until our present level of maturity in Christ, we have been taught to **declare** that Jesus is Lord.

But, do we really understand what we are saying? Do we really know in spirit and in truth that He is Lord, or have we just accepted this saying without question? And, if these words are true, do we know why they are true? In other words, do we honor these words in heart, or do they just habitually and thoughtlessly pour out of our mouths like a catchy Christian mantra? Do we honor them in spirit, or are they just Christian "lingo" used like a password at a social club or secular organization to let others know we are part of the holy in-crowd? Are they words legalistically uttered as part of a religious rite, or are they an expression of submission to our high and humble Lord?

Whatever our reasons for our declaration, these words, Jesus Christ is Lord, represent absolute truth. There is no bona fide challenge to either their content or accuracy. **Jesus Christ** and no other One, past, present, or future, is Lord. Jesus **is** now, presently, at this very moment in our lives, our unique Lord. Jesus is **Lord**, the One with the right to rule, reign, lead, guide, be Master of, and Sovereign over us.

Thankfully the proof of such powerful proclamations is impregnated throughout the Bible. When searched for, it is not a once mentioned, soon forgotten footnote of Scripture but rather a dominant theme of the Word. Since it is repeated over and over again in both the Old and New Testaments, its significance cannot be missed or minimized. In ascertaining that

Jesus Is Lord, there are keys to open the doors of our heart. We begin in the book of Matthew.

Toward the end of His life as a Man among men on earth Jesus was confronted by a group of Pharisees, one of whom asked Him, "*Teacher, which is the great commandment in the Law?*" (Matthew 22:36). To answer him, Jesus quoted scripture from the books of Deuteronomy and Leviticus. *is the great commandment in the Law?*" (Matthew 22:36). To answer him, Jesus quoted scripture from the books of Deuteronomy and Leviticus.

Then, continuing the conversation with the religious leaders, He used their own format, questions, to challenge them. Wanting them to acknowledge His holy and legitimate authority, He asked them, "*What do you think about the Christ, whose son is He?*" (verse 42).

Put on the spot to publicly disclose their thoughts for or against Him, in a predicament where they were being asked to acknowledge or deny His right to rule them, they tried to sidestep Jesus' question. To answer Him, they said He was, "*…the son of David.*" (verse 42).

But Jesus jumped on this answer. Using their own words and their own scripture, He boldly pummeled them with some of David's own words.

> *Jesus said to them, "Then how does David in the Spirit call Him 'Lord,' saying, 'THE LORD SAID TO MY LORD, "SIT AT MY RIGHT HAND, UNTIL I PUT THINE ENEMIES BENEATH THY FEET'?" Matthew 22:43,44*

He ended the challenge by asking a final question that they could not or would not answer.

> *"If David then calls Him 'Lord,' how is He his son?" Matthew 22:45*

Or, to paraphrase, how could He, Jesus, be a mere son of man, a son of David if David, one of the greatest men who ever lived, called Him Lord?

To understand the quandary Jesus had the Pharisees in, we must turn to scripture. As David loved God, so God loved him. The New Testament says that the horn of salvation would come from the house of David (Luke 1:69). Indeed, it did!

David was a man after God's own heart (Acts 13:22). As shepherd, in his quiet hours, he delighted in God; as warrior, he brought victory and peace through God; as leader, he was a man of mighty deeds and exploits who retired to his harp to express his unending love for God; as ruler and king, he governed all Israel and established worship as the primary means of relationship with God.

Additionally, David is also the Bible's best known psalmist. It was he who, at various ages and various stages of life, wrote and sang dozens of songs. Though at times the deeper meaning of his words may seem obscure, it is from some of these psalms that information is gleaned which conclusively proves that Jesus is Lord. And though it is sometimes difficult to decipher who is being spoken of, it is from David's songs that we are given the keys to understand why He is Lord.

KEY 1:

The revelation of eternal leadership from the house of David.

At some time in David's life, God vowed that He would place one of David's descendants on David's throne. And, if his sons would remain faithful and obedient to God, that promise was eternal.

> *The LORD has sworn to David, a truth from which He will not turn back; "Of the fruit of your body I will set upon your throne. If your sons will keep My covenant, and My testimony which I will teach them, their sons also shall sit upon your throne forever." Psalm 132:11,12.*

Yet another psalm reveals more. After God revealed a hidden truth to him, David prophetically spoke forth the definitive sign that would separate this eternal ruler from all others.

> *I have set the LORD continually before me; because He is at my right hand, I will not be shaken. Therefore my heart is glad, and my glory rejoices; my flesh also will swell securely. For Thou wilt not abandon my soul to Sheol; neither wilt Thou allow Thy Holy One to undergo decay. Psalm 16:8-10*

These visionary words indicate that David had entered into an extraordinary relationship with God. If we look deeper, they also reveal some startling facts:

1. A seed of David, a descendant from his own loins, would occupy his throne.

2. Because of this descendant, the throne of David would last forever. The one who ruled from it would rule forever.

3. This of course was impossible for a man who is subject to physical limitations.

4. Therefore God was speaking of a divine Seed, an eternal King, a holy Man not forever subject to the physical limitation of death.

5. The acceptable sign for this King, that which declared that He and no other as the future Sovereign was that He would not be abandoned in death. He would die, but unlike all other men, His body would not decay or corrupt. In other words, though He would die, He would yet live to rule eternally.

So powerful and far reaching a promise was this that it was declared to be a covenant between David and God. Confirmation of this comes from another psalmist, Ethan.

> *"I have made a covenant with My chosen; I have sworn to David My servant, I will establish your seed forever, and build up your throne for all generations." Psalm 89:3,4*

KEY 2:

The exaltation of the future ruler from the house of David.

While these three scriptures from the book of Psalms give a glimpse of and guide us toward general recognition of the future Lord, it is another psalm that specifically identifies Him. When David first uttered the words of Psalm 110:1, he was in essence calling Jesus Lord.

> *The LORD says to my Lord: "Sit at My right hand, until I make Thine enemies a footstool for Thy feet."*

According to the Greek translation, when David said, "*The LORD says to my Lord*", he was saying, "Jehovah says to my Adonai". Because he used the pronoun, my, David was declaring that he had an Adonai or Lord. Essentially, in the initial phrase of this verse, God or the Father is speaking to the One who David recognized and acknowledged as His own personal Lord. He was addressing the One who was of David's line but yet a divine Ruler and holy Sovereign.

David whose lot was to be head over men, whose training was to be ruler and king, whose preparation as a shepherd facing lion and bear and whose status as a warrior either fighting Israel's enemies or as a fugitive fleeing from Saul made him a leader of leaders and a lord of lords in his own right was declaring that he had a Lord. This man who could rise no farther in the world, this king who could ascend no higher in life was quick and free to acknowledge that there was One much more highly exalted than he, the Lord of lords to whom he bowed.

Such was the absence of jealousy and selfish ambition, such was the testimony of the love and grace God had placed in David's heart that it was not hard for him, a king, to submit to the King; it was not difficult for him, an extraordinary leader of men to revere the Leader of men. Instead, it was an honor for him, a lord with authority over the lives of the people of Israel, to reveal and direct attention to the Lord with dominion over all.

Too, from this scripture, when it says, *"Sit at My right hand until I make Your enemies a footstool for Your feet"*, the LORD was saying to David's Lord, "Ascend to My throne and assume power". Because in Old Testament times the ruling posture was to sit (such as Eli sitting by the gate to await news of the battle in 1 Samuel 4:13 or Boaz negotiating to marry Ruth in Ruth 4:1), Father was saying to Son, *"Be seated in the place of authority and rule. Assume the position of King and lead. Be sovereign Lord on My throne until I vanquish Your enemies."* (See also 1 Corinthians 15:25; Colossians 3:1; Hebrews 12:2).

Surely now the identity of this Lord is clear. David saw the Lord of all. Specifically, he had divine revelation of the life, suffering, crucifixion, death, resurrection, ascension, and exaltation of one of his descendants. In all of history, there is only One who lived as a Man among men, only One who suffered and died for them, only One whose flesh did not decompose or decay in death, only One who was so sovereignly resurrected from death never to die again by the power of God, only One who was raised and then seated at the right hand of God to rule eternally. This One was David's Lord. He is our Lord. He is the Lord, Jesus Christ.

This Adonai David knew by promise of God. This Adonai David saw by prophetic insight. This Adonai met the full requirement to be Lord. This Adonai David declared with his own heart and voice to be Lord. So must we.

For those who prefer more modern scriptures, there is dramatic confirmation of this divine identification in the New Covenant. In an event that remains unique in the history of mankind, one supernatural being appeared on earth to announce the birth and mission of another supernatural Being. When the angel, Gabriel, was sent to an espoused virgin, he said:

"Do not be afraid, Mary, for you have found favor with God. And behold, you will conceive in your womb, and bear a son, and you shall name Him Jesus. He will be great, and will be called the Son of the Most High; and the Lord God will give Him the throne of His father David; And He will reign over the house of Jacob forever, and His kingdom will have no end." Luke 1:30- 33

This maiden had found blessing in God and the announced fruit of that blessing was a Son. By divine proclamation, this Son was to be named Jesus, He was declared to be the Son of God, He was to be given the throne of David, and His rule was to last forever.

In later years, God again used these same scriptures to establish both the position and authority of Jesus as Lord among those who did not know it.

Peter was one who used David's words to prove that Jesus is Lord. To him, after the stunning and shattering events in Jerusalem during which Jesus was betrayed, murdered, and then raised from the dead to ascend into heaven, David's prophecies had been fulfilled. When Peter explained these events, he gave a third key to help us understand our Lord. Unlike the other two keys which identify Jesus as Lord, this third key tells why He is Lord.

The LORD will perfect that which concerns me; Psalm 138:8 NJKV

∞

Chapter 8

Why Jesus is Lord

My Lord and my God.   John 20:28

In addition to the revelation and the exaltation of the future ruler from the house of David, there is another key to understanding why Jesus is Lord.

KEY 3:

The sovereignty of God.

By Peter's testimony, Jesus had told His disciples to wait in Jerusalem for the promise of the Father. On the day of Pentecost, the promise—or the Holy Spirit—came. Accompanied by a supernatural force of wind and unusual displays of fire, the disciples were filled with this Spirit. As a result, their tongues were so changed or loosened that the multi-national pilgrims gathered in the city for the holy feast were amazed to hear uneducated Galileans speaking to them in their own native languages. It was when some began to mock and accuse the disciples of drunkenness that Peter seized the moment to extol Jesus (Acts 2).

Initially, he quoted the prophet Joel who spoke of supernatural conditions that would affect mankind and nature in the last days (verses 16-21). And then, he introduced Jesus into the conversation. Speaking to the Jews, he cited Jesus as a miracle worker (verse 22) and declared that, "*...this Man, delivered up by the predetermined plan and foreknowledge of God you nailed to the cross by the hands of godless men and put Him to death.*" (verse 23).

Peter began to incorporate the keys by which Jesus is identified as Lord into his message. Continuing to speak, he said, *"And God raised Him up again, putting an end to the agony of death since it was impossible for Him to be held in its power"* (verse 24). Using scripture as proof of his comments, Peter quoted David:

> *"FOR DAVID SAYS OF HIM, "I WAS ALWAYS BEHOLDING THE LORD IN MY PRESENCE; FOR HE IS AT MY RIGHT HAND, THAT I MAY NOT BE SHAKEN. THEREFORE MY HEART WAS GLAD AND MY TONGUE EXULTED; MOREOVER MY FLESH ALSO WILL ABIDE IN HOPE; BECAUSE THOU WILT NOT ABANDON MY SOUL TO HADES NOR ALLOW THY HOLY ONE TO UNDERGO DECAY."" ACTS 2:25-27*

To make it very clear that in quoting David he was not referring to David, Peter then made a pointed contrast. When David had died and was buried, he had not been raised by God to rule again either on earth or in heaven; his tomb was still there (verse 29). On the other hand, when Jesus whose ancestry through the house and line of David is traced in Matthew 1 and Luke 3 died, He did not stay dead. He was not left in Sheol and His flesh did not see corruption. Instead it was He, Jesus, who was resurrected by God and exalted to the right hand of the Father and He who is seated in glory while His enemies are made His footstool.

*"**This** Jesus God raised up again..." (verse 32) (emphasis mine)*

Then quoting the now familiar verse in Psalm 110:1, Peter spoke the words that end all argument as to who is Lord and why. Adding his own caveat to words of Scripture, he proclaimed that a sovereign act of God established Jesus as Lord. In words that thundered to the devout in Jerusalem and reverberate through the corridors of time to the church today, he announced the intervention of God into things human and holy. Describing an act of God that no man can disregard or undo, Peter proclaimed:

"Therefore let all the house of Israel know for certain that
God has made this Jesus *whom you crucified*
*both **Lord** and Christ. Acts 2:36; NKJV (emphasis mine)*

God did not make David Lord. He did not make any other giant of the Old Testament Lord. God did not make Peter Lord. He did not make anyone listening to Peter that day Lord. He did not make any other New Testament personalities Lord. God did not make us Lord.

But, by a divine act, in an exercise of His ultimate, supreme authority, by the uncontested power of His Being, in His unlimited greatness, God made Him—Jesus—Lord. Jesus is Lord because all powerful, almighty God made Him Lord.

Even as Jesus once confronted religious leaders in an attempt to get them to acknowledge He was Lord, so now He may be challenging us, "What do you think about the Christ, whose son is He?"

Are we like the Pharisees who had trouble acknowledging that the one they perceived only as a man was in truth their Lord? Or, are we among those who understand that the name LORD means Jesus is the very essence of life. Faced with death, He gave Himself to death to conquer death and was then raised from the dead. He is no longer on the cross. He is no longer in the tomb. He is risen, glorified, exalted into heaven, crowned as Lord and now rules in heaven from the very throne of God. He is alive, the LORD of life, and from His position of victory, gives, maintains and sustains our lives.

Are we among those who understand that the title Lord means Jesus is a strong, powerful Sovereign, Master of all creation, Ruler of all nations and peoples, the One given all authority, "..in heaven and on earth" (Matthew 28:18)? Do we acknowledge that seated in the position of authority at the right hand of God, the place of power, He is prophecy fulfilled?

None other is so honored. No other meets the requirement. This Jesus is the descendant of David. This Jesus suffered and died. This Jesus was resurrected by God and ascended into heaven. This Jesus was exalted into eternal kingship by God. This Jesus was made Lord by God. Whether we like it or not, whether we agree with it or not, whether we acknowledge it or not, this Jesus is Lord because God, by an exercise of sovereign power, made Him Lord.

"…if you confess with your mouth Jesus as Lord, and believe in your heart that God raised Him from the dead, you shall be saved;" Romans 10:9

ॐ

Chapter 9

Paul's Open Veil

"...our sole Master and Lord, Jesus Christ (the Messiah, the Anointed One)." Jude 4; AMP

The Old Testament objectively teaches that the LORD, Jehovah, and the Lord, Adonai, are the same divine Being, the One we call Jesus. It also recounts the subjective experience of the prophet, Isaiah, who saw Him through the Open Veil. The New Testament follows suit. It objectively identifies its Kurios or Lord as Jesus and describes events in another man's life who subjectively experienced the Lord by seeing and hearing through the Open Veil. His name is Paul.

Paul, once known as Saul, is a man who by his own testimony was, *"a Jew, born in Tarsus of Cilicia, but brought up in this city, educated under Gamaliel, strictly according to the law of our fathers, being zealous for God..."* (Acts 22:3). Further, of himself he states that he was, *"circumcised the eighth day, of the nation of Israel, ...a Hebrew of Hebrews; as to the Law, a Pharisee; as to zeal, a persecutor of the church; as to the righteousness which is in the Law, found blameless" (Philippians 3:5,6).* Though he was born a Roman citizen, he was a member of the Jewish Council (Acts 22:28; 26:10). Moreover, by his own evaluation, he was an accuser, tyrant, torturer, pursuer, and persecutor.

Paul served God through a form of religion, becoming a fanatic in his desire to impose the legalism of rite, ceremony, tradition, and formality upon all around him. His "love" for God included everything from terrorizing and imprisoning any who deviated from religious law even a little to overseeing the death of those judged as outright defectors. In blind hatred of those he thought had abused his religious tradition, he especially set his sights against Christians or followers of The Way, the disciples of the Lord, Jesus Christ.

When the church began to increase in number, when more and more Jews were breaking ranks to follow the Lord, when leaders in Jewish congregations were losing long-held control over people's lives, when religious leaders were no longer followed and treated as near gods, Paul grew incensed. Breathing fire, he obtained the legal right to undertake intense persecution of Christians.

The story is detailed in Acts 9. Even from the outset, while exacting vengeance on human beings, this stubborn and hateful Paul knew he was on a collision course with the Lord. *"Now Saul, still breathing threats and murder against the disciples of the Lord, went to the high priest"* (Acts 9:1).

Not content to pursue his murderous ways or to restrict his horror to Jerusalem, he sought to expand his reign of terror to other cities. His intent was to legally evict those he judged as miscreants and to bring them back to Jerusalem for torture and possible death (verse 2).

On a trip to do just that, on a venture to pursue Christians and forcefully drag them back to Jerusalem, he approached the city of Damascus. And suddenly it happened! Into this scene of stark terror, rage, evil, intimidation and out-of-control hatred, the glorious presence of God broke into his life. The Lord he despised met him. As scripture tells the story,

> *"And it came about that as he journeyed, he was approaching Damascus, and suddenly a light from heaven flashed around him..."* Acts 9:3

.

Paul's eyes were opened and he saw a light. It was neither human light as from a torch nor a natural, earthly light as that coming from the sun. He instantly knew that this light which was encircling and encompassing him was from heaven.

Paul's response to the supernatural vision is also recorded:

"...and he fell to the ground" (verse 9:4)

So awed, so overcome, so startled was he that his instant reaction was to fall off his horse.

The confrontation continued:

"...and heard a voice saying to him, "Saul, Saul, why are you persecuting Me?"

First, his supernatural eyes were open to see the unusual. Now, his ears were unplugged, too. Though there were others with him, a commanding voice specifically addressed Saul and succinctly cut to the heart of the issue. The question asked him wasn't, "Why are you terrorizing men and women, humans, or your neighbors?" It wasn't even, "Why are you persecuting Christians?" The voice Saul heard revealingly asked, "Why are you harrying, harassing, badgering, tormenting Me?"

Paul, astounded as he must have been, was yet able to muster the strength and boldness to ask a question of his own: *"Who art Thou, Lord?" (Acts 9:5)*

Saul wasn't asking this question because he didn't know who had stopped him. His own words identify his Confronter. He didn't ask the supernatural voice a generic, "Who are you?" and then wait for the answer. He specifically queried, *"Who are You, Lord?"* Like Isaiah before him who in his own encounter with the divine knew he was in the presence of the LORD, so Paul instantly knew he was in the presence of the Lord. Without explanation or any word of introduction, he knew this was the Lord---and he addressed Him as such.

And quickly, the Lord confirmed Paul's insight:

And He said, "I am Jesus whom you are persecuting…(verse 5)

Did we catch that? Do we really grasp the profound impact of these words? After Paul had correctly identified and acknowledged the One speaking to him as the Lord, the veil was drawn back on more truth. In response to Paul's specific question, He said, *"I am Jesus…"*. In using the words , "I am", the Lord was identifying Himself to be Jehovah, LORD of the Old Covenant, too. In other words, He was declaring that the One receiving worship as Lord, Adonai or Kurios, and the One bringing life out of death, Jehovah, was Jesus.

In three small but immeasurably powerful words the course of history was changed. By them the course of Paul's life was transformed, too. It was Paul, now the instrument of God, who was sent out to spread the revelation of the Lordship of Jesus Christ to the first century Jews and Gentiles. It was also Paul who went on to write the good news in his Epistles that fill so much of the New Testament. And it is Paul, by words that still thunder down through the ages, who has brought men into right relationship with the Lord Jesus for the last two centuries

Paul saw a heavenly sight. He heard supernatural sound. When God broke into his life, rearranged his plans, literally knocked him off his high horse and brought him into personal encounter with the Lord Paul experienced his Open Veil.

Isaiah loved the Lord and served Him. Paul hated the Lord and persecuted Him. Both Isaiah and Paul saw the Lord. Isaiah saw the delights of heaven. Paul saw the Light from heaven. He was brought into the light of under-standing and acceptance by the Light of the world. Isaiah heard seraphim. Paul both heard and talked to the Lord. Though their lives and circumstances were so very different, God blessed both men with a supernatural experience revealing His Person to them; He drew back the veil.

As He had done for Isaiah, God lifted the veil that keeps mankind enclosed in and encompassed by the earthly realm. Responding to this miraculous initiation, Saul entered into the heavenly and divine. God allowed another man who until then could only gain information from his limited, finite physical senses to overcome the restrictions of the human body by sovereignly quickening his supernatural senses: Saul saw supernatural light and heard supernatural sound. Too, God allowed another man bound and overbalanced by the processes of logic, reason, and analysis to overcome the inadequacies of the human mind so that he "knew" in his spirit. Paul knew Jesus was Lord.

And, like Isaiah, Paul's encounter with the Open Veil met with some remarkable results. The first fruit was death.

Paul's death was not the slow, painful, lingering kind. Rather it was instant capitulation. Death to the past, death to unholy goals, dreams and aspirations. Death to the leadership impelled by hatred. Death to rage, terror, and persecution. Death to self and his whole way of life.

This former fire breathing zealot of zealots who hated Christians and the Christ they worshipped was completely undone and forever changed by this one glimpse of glory. In one instant of death to self, God changed darkness to light, hatred to love, and fanaticism to obedience, all so that His will could be done through this man.

The second result of the Open Veil experience was life. God healed Paul. The eyes that were blinded by hatred now had vision. At the sight of the Light, though physically blinded temporarily, Paul could, maybe for the first time ever, see. The ears that had been deaf to the cries of terror and pleas for mercy could now hear. Out of the din and cacophony of the fright and pain of the many unheard voices once raised to plead with him, he could now hear one voice. Maybe for the first time ever, he heard the right voice.

In later days when Paul had been seized in the temple and was recounting this supernatural incident to Jews, he added another nugget of truth. After Jesus had identified Himself, Paul asked another question.

> *"And those who were with me beheld the light, to be sure, but did not understand the voice of the One who was speaking to me. And I said, 'What shall I do, Lord?'" Acts 22:9,10*

This time he wasn't seeking a name or the confirmation of an identity; he was submitting to higher authority. Over his own authority and power, he was acknowledging Jesus as Leader, Master, Sovereign. He was declaring His right to rule. And he was declaring His right to rule Paul. From the first moment that Jesus revealed Himself, Paul was no longer his own man. He fully and completely belonged to Jesus.

When healed of the temporary blindness, a disciple named Ananias told him:

> *And he said, 'The God of our fathers has appointed you to know His will, and to see the Righteous One, and to hear an utterance from His mouth. For you will be a witness for Him to all men of what you have seen and heard." (Acts 22:14,15)*

Later when Jesus told him that He would, "*...send you far away to the Gentiles...* " (verse 21), Paul began living for rather than dying toward the Lord. He rose up, obeyed, and the rest is history. The Open Veil galvanized him into a ministry that changed the entire world.

"Who are You, Lord?" "What shall I do, Lord?" Acts 22:8,10

Chapter 10
Our Open Veil

This hope we have as an anchor of the soul, a hope both sure and steadfast and one which enters within the veil, where Jesus has entered as a forerunner for us.... Hebrews 6:19,20

Is it stretching the permissible boundaries of mind, soul, and spirit to declare that as Isaiah saw the Lord who was high and lifted up and heard the seraphim serenade Him, and as Paul experienced the Open Veil and saw the Light and talked with the Lord, so we too can have an Open Veil experience? In truth, each of us who are reborn spiritually (and by God's sovereign grace some who are not) can experience the Open Veil, the place where God transcends our humanity, we enter the supernatural and we meet the Lord. As part of our covenant, the way has already been made.

Long ago when the Hebrews had escaped from Egypt, God told their leader, Moses, to build a tabernacle. Of three parts, a curtain was to separate the Outer Court from the second court, the Holy Place. Another inner curtain or veil was to separate the Holy Place from the third chamber, the Holy of Holies. Specific instructions were given concerning the formation of that inner curtain.

"And you shall make a veil of blue and purple and scarlet material and fine twisted linen; it shall be made with cherubim, the work of a skill-ful workman. And you shall hang it on four pillars of acacia overlaid with gold, their hooks also being of gold, on four sockets of silver. And you shall hang up the veil under the clasps, and shall bring in the ark of the testimony there within the veil; and the veil shall serve for you as a partition between the holy place and the Holy of Holies. Exodus 26:31-33

When later dwelling places for God were built, they followed the original pattern of courts and curtains. Even in Herod's Temple, existing in Jerusalem when Jesus walked its byways, the Holy Place or court where the priests ministered to God, and the Most Holy Place which held the ark which symbolized the presence of God were divided or separated by a curtain.

Two thousand years ago, sovereign God mightily and graciously blessed men by the power of His Holy Spirit. He planned and oversaw the birth of a baby whose name was Jesus. God in human form, Jesus lived and grew among men.

But there was something different about Jesus. Though He lived among sinful people in exceedingly corrupt and difficult times, He never sinned. No matter the situation, no matter the circumstance, whether in word, thought, deed or attitude, Jesus never missed the mark or entered lawlessness. No sin touched Him, clung to Him, or was committed by Him, He was totally unblemished (Hebrews 7:26).

Not only was His life unequaled, but His purpose in life was singular, too. Though sinless, He came as a love offering to die for the sins of men. He came to earth and lived as a man specifically, at a time of His Father's choosing, to take on His perfect Person all the sins of all men and to suffer and die for them.

And suffer He did! In ways the depths of which cannot be plumbed, in ways the horror of which cannot by understood or told, He was tortured unto death. As the sweet, holy, pure sacrifice, as the innocent Lamb of God, He shed His blood and died, offering Himself as the only sacrifice worthy or able to redeem mankind from sin.

The blessings from Jesus' death and subsequent resurrection are not limited to the forgiveness of sin. Magnificent as that is, the riches are even more numerous. One other blessing coming out of His sacrifice is the provision of the Open Veil.

Scripture tells us that Jesus' death was not an ordinary one. Extraordinary purpose was accompanied by astonishing events. The supernatural broke forth. Unholy powers of evil were loosed to accomplish and mock His death; the power of God was loosed to honor it.

After His holy death, the laws of nature were overcome. The earth shook. Rocks were split. Tombs of the dead were opened, the dead raised to life and, entering the streets of Jerusalem, were seen by many (Matthew 27:51-53).

While earthly nature was convulsing at the death of Jesus, so was human nature. Soldiers were frightened; people were filled with awe; multitudes who had gathered for the spectacle began to repent and beat their breasts in sorrow. Even the Centurion, the Roman officer (and a Gentile!) overseeing the event testified, "*Truly, this was the Son of God!*" (Matthew 27:54; Luke 23:47).

But what one special occurrence followed the death of Jesus yet preceded these supernatural outbursts of power? What single non-human, supernatural phenomenon happened that announced the Lamb's death and set in motion this display of godly mourning?

> *And Jesus cried out again with a loud voice, and yielded up His spirit. And behold, the veil of the temple was torn in two from top to bottom... Matthew 27: 50,51*

That this veil was split is not a hidden, trivial footnote of history. That it is mentioned in three gospel accounts (Matthew 27:51; Mark 15:38; Luke

23:45) before other details of the aftermath of the crucifixion makes it extremely significant. It is a primary fruit of His blessings.

As described in the word of God, this veil was torn in a specific way: "*…torn in two from top to bottom.*" An accomplishment of no mere man, this veil was destroyed by the hand of God Himself. This curtain once commanded to be made by God was now ripped asunder by God giving man access to God.

In Moses' Tabernacle, if the veil had been ripped and access given to the Holy of Holies, priests ministering to God, if they had lived through the experience, would have seen the Ark of the Covenant and the Mercy Seat, the place of God's glory. But when Jesus died and the veil in Herod's temple was split completely in two, men could see God. Those who would be New Covenant priests were given permission, an invitation was issued, and their way was made—through the Open Veil—to enter into the very presence of their Most Holy God.

In other words, the veil that kept priests near God but not in His presence was torn in two. The veil separating the Holy Place of ministry from the holiest place of worship was destroyed. The veil which allowed men to minister **for** God but not **before** Him was cast aside. Now men could enter the Holy of Holies through the Open Veil. They could see Him face to face. They could find themselves not in the presence of a piece of furniture but in the presence of the holy, living God. And they could fall at His feet and worship Him.

There is much more to the Open Veil than can be seen or understood in the natural realm. This one part of the overall event we know as the crucifixion has profound spiritual implications for all men. Tearing aside the veil was God's invitation to enter in. By so doing, God was casting aside every hindrance, removing every restriction, and destroying every excuse that kept men from right and intimate relationship with Him. He made way for whosoever will to run into His open arms. "Whosoever will" includes us.

Surely this is good news for sinners. Born in sin and under authority of Satan, their minds, similar to those of Old Testament Jews, are hardened against God. When Scripture is read or referred to, there is no understanding because a veil blocks the truth. When they see holiness and godliness shining out of others who have been in the presence of God, they are offended and demand that this glory be covered (2 Corinthians 3:13-15).

But no one has to stay in this condition. No one must remain veiled, blinded, alienated. God, in His holy grace, loves those who do not love Him. He has already reached out to all through His Son, Jesus. Even as any will accept His sacrifice, open his heart to the Lord, believe in Him, and call on His name, the veil of separation is removed (2 Corinthians 3:16).

All who respond to God's invitation to salvation are immediately showered with His blessings. The veil's destruction results in the mind's new acceptance of the Bible as inerrant truth and in deeper understanding of things holy. Each new saint is drawn to rather than repulsed by the sight and presence of God.

Yet there is more!

Now the Lord is the Spirit; and where the Spirit of the Lord is, there is liberty. 2 Corinthians 3:17

The Spirit of the Lord indwells the newly quickened spirit of man and brings freedom from the bondage of sin, releasing each from the now illegal authority of Satan over his life, from residence in the kingdom of darkness, from this present evil age and from flesh. It brings the liberty of choice that Jesus be Lord.

And another blessing is transformation.

But we all, with unveiled face beholding as in a mirror the glory of the Lord, are being transformed into the same image from glory to glory, just as from the Lord, the Spirit.   2 Corinthians 3:18

When newly reborn, clean, and beautiful, every new lamb is given the chance to grow and change. With no veils to block, restrict, or deny him access, he can see the glory of the Lord and be transformed, conformed and changed into that same image by the Spirit now resident within him.

So complete the metamorphosis that each, by invitation and delight of God, can confidently and trustingly enter the courts of ministry unto God. By way of the blood, through the veil of His flesh, each, with sincere heart, new faith and cleansed conscience, can draw near to love and serve Him (Hebrews 10:19-22).

While the Open Veil delights new saints, its blessings belong to those already walking with Him, too. It never stops revealing more of the Lord to any who want to see—and it keeps the way open for those who long to enter the Holy of Holies.

For some, salvation was a long ago event. Days, months, years of growth and change followed. Somewhere along the way, many took seriously the admonition to serve the Lord and, whether personally or through a religious organization, began to do so.

If individually involved in ministry, those some would call laymen, time and commitment are always challenges. Life gets crowded. Responsibilities at home and on the job increase. Sometimes everyday life begins to crowd out the Bread of Life. And a veil ever so slowly and ever so subtly raises which separates the earnest, hard working saint from fuller relationship with God.

Others following the path of denominationally prescribed ministry suffer similar trials and temptations. Becoming deeply involved in assigned tasks and overly busy with church hierarchy, organization, meetings, departments, committees, and just plain "doing the stuff", they find themselves lodged in that holy place of ministry but not in the higher, holiest place of rest and worship. The one is termed (sometimes with resentment on the part of the overworked minister) as working for God; the other is enjoying Him.

Functioning out of a good intention, genuinely helping the body of Christ, openly involved in the work of the church which they truly desired and trained for, they lose touch with the One they are supposedly ministering to. Concerned with good works, good causes and looking good, these are not aware of the almost inevitable moment that the change is made from being led by God to obeying man; they aren't able to recognize the season when serving man has taken precedence over serving the Lord.

Stretched to the limit, busy day and night, faced with piles, loads, and stacks of assignments before them, they don't know that a curtain has arisen behind them. Overwhelmingly deluged with Holy Place ministry to men rather than beautifully, gloriously immersed in Holy of Holy ministry before God, they are separated from God, near but not in His presence. God who was once seen and delighted in as Best Friend, now seems far away.

For these, too, the curtain has been torn. For these precious ones, the veil has been ripped away. Nothing truly separates the priests of God from the presence of God except a choice: to continue to grind it out by flesh, performance, works, duties and the search for perfection---or to enter His rest. If they discover anew that Jesus, not their present job description, title or ministry, is their God and Jesus, not their agenda or their workload, is their Lord, then they too can walk through the Open Veil. They too can enter the deepest, central chamber, the Holy of Holies, and find joy in His presence and delight in His worship. And as their focus adjusts to His bright light, they find there is much to do here in, not near, the presence of God. Their service of worship, once a good idea, is now a God idea.

Does any of this sound familiar? Does it describe our situations? Can we change some of the *theys* to *we*? Be reassured! No matter our time of life, no matter our place or circumstances, for all, by the grace, mercy and blessing of Jesus Christ, the veil has been torn away. Whether it concerns the revelation of Jesus Christ as Lord for salvation or the revelation of Jesus Christ as Lord for sanctification and service, our way has been made to God. Through the Open Veil, He stands with open arms waiting to receive us.

Like Isaiah and Paul, each of us can have an Open Veil experience. All of us can leave our present circumstances, enter the throne room of God, die that we may live, and have our lives changed forever.

The LORD your God in your midst, the Mighty One, will save; He will rejoice over you with gladness, He will quiet you in His love, He will rejoice over you with singing. Zephaniah 3:17; NKJV

Chapter 11

What is the Open Veil?

How blessed are the people who know the joyful sound! O LORD, they walk in the light of Thy countenance. Psalm 89:15

Scripture, in both Old Testament and New, has revealed a sovereign Lord whose name is Jesus. It has also detailed special occurrences or "Open Veil" experiences in the lives of men which have permanently changed them in the very heart of their beings. Further, it has taught that this Lord, Jesus Christ, through His own death and resurrection, has made the way for every born-again saint to welcome and participate in such an event. If we want to walk through the Open Veil, we must, from both objective fact and subjective experience, more clearly understand what the Open Veil is.

First, it must be made clear that the Open Veil is....

NOT a human whim, but an event designed and planned by God.

NOT a haughty command to God, but a delight initiated by God.

NOT a work of flesh or a demonic counterfeit of things holy, but a miraculous and divine intervention into human law and life.

Thus, initiated by the Lord, the Open Veil is an act of grace freely given through the Spirit of God as a blessing to men of His choosing in ways of His choosing for reasons of His choosing.

The Open Veil is invitation into His presence.

- It is our personal invitation to step into the Holy of Holies and be with God.

- It is His personal request, bidding or summons that we join Him in His chambers.

- It is joining Him where He is and becoming immersed in His Being.

- It is dwelling with Him as He has dwelt with us.

The Open Veil is revelation.

- The Open Veil is our personal revelation of the Lord. This disclosure of the holy can be a sudden revelation as in the cases of Isaiah and Paul where their whole beings were immediately and fiercely committed to and consumed by the glory of the Lord. Or, it can be a long process of disclosure in which God continuously unveils parts of His exaltation in ever increasing ways and power so we are, step by step, moved from spark to flame to fire to on fire in our delight in Him. Finally, by God's sovereign choice, the means of the encounter can be a combination of the two.

- The Open Veil is that time and place where supernatural senses are activated by God, not man or the demonic, so saints can see, hear, or otherwise experience the sights and sounds of heaven and know the Lord who resides and rules there.

- The Open Veil is humbled awareness of the wide chasm that can separate Creator and creation: His love for us and ours for ourselves, His desire for us and ours for ourselves, the intent of His heart toward us and ours toward ourselves, His power towards us to bring His will to pass in us and our learning we are totally unable to help ourselves. It is also the confidence that in spite of the immeasurable gulf of heart (not of salvation), He will love us into His desire for us as He draws us unto Himself.

- The Open Veil is learning of the majesty and power, the honor and excellence of the Lord, a blessing which does not come by analysis, reasoning, logic or imagination but rather by the divine revelation of the Spirit of God.

- The Open Veil is the continuous entwining of hearts, holy and human, until we one day realize there truly is no greater purpose in life than to love this Lord our God with all our heart, soul, strength, mind, body, and being.

- The Open Veil is growing thankfulness to our Lord not for what He will give us or what we can get from Him, but for who He is.

- The Open Veil is the powerful and on-going awareness of our relationship to the Awesome and Jealous God whose power could have crushed us, but He loved us; whose leadership could have misled us, but He guided us; whose mastery could have enslaved us, but He served us; whose ownership could have stripped us of life, but He gave us courage and confidence to go on—in Him.

- The Open Veil is preparation and release into new life—by death.

The Open Veil is death.

- The Open Veil is the circumstances by which self is demolished by slow or sudden understanding, and the recognition, and acknowledgment that He is Lord. It is God leading us, much like those on the road to Emmaus, to see the Lord and purposefully using the details (good or bad) and situations involved in that need of revelation (pleasant or painful) to bring us into deeper and closer relationship with the Lord.

- The Open Veil is being as the soldiers in awe of Him, like the people repenting before Him, and the centurion praising Him, all in brokenness.

- The Open Veil is an encounter with Truth which slays forever traditional religious beliefs and unholy human commands and demands when His absolute standard is raised.

- The Open Veil is the place of conviction, confession, forgiveness, and healing. It is a blessing of such unforgettable magnitude and such everlasting impact that lives are forever changed and those so changed delight to have it so.

- The Open Veil is the overwhelming relief at the release from our self-appointed jobs as leader, master, ruler of our own lives (and often, sadly, the lives of those around us). It is our removal from His throne and once in our rightful place, our growing joy as He reigns in our lives. It is the journey from the unconfessed fear and pressure of leading our own lives to the security and peace found in trusting and following the true Leader.

- The Open Veil is acknowledging our weakness and admitting that our only strength is in Him. It is casting our weaknesses into His strength.

- The Open Veil is the cessation of and death to works of flesh, and the pressures, striving, struggling, and pushiness that constantly affirm that we are not yet like the Father. It is laying down personal desires, dreams, goals, ambitions, busyness, and if need be even ministries and refusing to war with Him about them anymore. It is sitting at His feet. It is accepting that He knows best and His plans for us are better than ours, His purposes for us more holy.

The Open Veil is life.

- The Open Veil is astonishment at His love for us.

- The Open Veil is understanding the higher place of the Lord even though we are one with Him. It is understanding the higher purposes of the Lord which He desires to accomplish through us.

- The Open Veil is inner change so overwhelmingly deep, so overpoweringly strong, so completely life transforming that we are never the same. The progressive or sudden recognition of Jesus as Lord tears away the cloudy dimness, the deceptions, and the errors of the past and brings us into clearly envisioned truth in the present. Often it gifts us with insight into the future.

- The Open Veil is responding with new life and joy when the Lord calls. It is entering the realm of the supernatural where, with the guidance of pillar and cloud, we follow Him beyond where we have gone before and, by the power of the arm of the Lord, we participate in what we have not experienced before. It is agreeing both to call Him Lord and to let Him be Lord.

- The Open Veil is increased awareness of being **a** light reflecting **the** Light. It is coming to understand that His divine declaration that we are the light of the world is not a command that we must guiltily struggle to keep as we yo-yo our way through various stages of light and darkness, strength and weakness, commitment and indifference. Rather, it is a prophetic proclamation which He brings to pass as He reveals more of His life to us and causes His light to shine on us, in us, and then through us to the dark world around us.

The Open Veil is hope for the future.

- The Open Veil is overwhelming awareness, reverence and awe of Sovereign Lord. It is growing intent to submit to this Master in every situation.

- The Open Veil is being so in love with the Lord that we want nothing more than to bow before Him and submit to and obey Him for the rest of our lives.

- The Open Veil is commitment. *"Here I am, Lord. Send me!"* (Isaiah 6:8)

- The Open Veil is entering in by learning the fullness of the phrase, *"Jesus is Lord!"* (Romans 10:9).

Which brings us to the Open Heaven.....

"Lord, I do believe; help my unbelief." Mark 9:24 (NKJV)

ℬℭ

Introduction to Part Two

The Open Heaven

Lift up your heads, O gates, and be lifted up, O ancient doors, that the King of glory may come in! Who is the King of glory? The LORD strong and mighty, the LORD mighty in battle. Lift up your heads, O gates, and lift them up, O ancient doors, that the King of glory may come in! Who is this King of glory? The LORD of hosts, He is the King of glory. Psalm 24:7-10

How blessed it is to know that Jesus is Lord! How comforting to know why He is Lord! How exciting it is to realize that each of us can, like Isaiah and Paul before us, anticipate the time, whether sudden or slow, subtle or dramatic, progressive or instantly powerful, when we know, agree and acknowledge that the Son of David is Sovereign Lord. And, whether initially or continuously, how delightful that all of us can yield to the deepening revelation that Jesus is our Lord!

But questions again arise. If we know that Jesus is Lord, what do we do with this truth? If we responded to the invitation to pass through the Open Veil into the presence of God, if we submitted to death and resurrection as a preparation, then we can legitimately ask, "Preparation for what?"

In the Bible there is a clear tension between knowing and doing. Some would describe this as the difference between objective knowledge and subjective experience. Others would see it in the differences of meaning in the scriptures, "...and you shall know (objective) that I am the LORD your

God... (Exodus 6:7), and "I am the good Shepherd; and I know My own and My own know (subjective) Me." (John 10:14).

As Christians, it is without question that we must learn about Christ. We learn about Him through the Word. Based on this Word, we are instructed about Him through classes, tapes, videos, books, seminars, sermons, and teaching retreats. While doctrine, theology, and intellectual objectivity are fine in their place, they are by no means all there is to Christianity. They are most assuredly not the only means of holy instruction.

As Christians, we are also commanded to know Christ. We aren't just to know about Him in our heads, but we are to enter into deep, personal, intimate relationship with Him in our hearts and spirits. This subjective "knowing" blooms through praise, worship, and prayer. And this subjective "knowing", whether from dreams, visions or the prophetic all must agree with and confirm the Word. By this knowing, the objective is counterbalanced by the subjective and faith leads to works.

For example, we may objectively know the facts that Jesus is the way, the truth and the life (John 14:6) and that He came to reveal the Father and to do His Father's will. But we can subjectively know Him only when we experience Jesus as the only path to the Father; we can subjectively know Him only when we walk with the One who models and speaks absolute truth to us; we can only subjectively know Him as we appropriate Him as our indwelling Life and the One who moves through us to bring life to others. We can only subjectively know Him when we allow Him to live through us and stretch us past the limits of our human minds to edify our spirits and to reveal God's will for us. Words are just words until the Word activates them in us and we allow them to govern and change our lives.

Perhaps James is best known for his comments about this. James was a brother of Jesus (Galatians. 1:19). Like so many others who first rejected Jesus as being extraordinary (Mark 3:21), he later became a believer (Acts 1:3,14). He even saw His brother as the risen Lord (1 Corinthians 15:7).

Surely therefore, he had the credentials to make this bold assertion: knowledge demands response; faith demands works.

> *Even so faith, if it has no works, is dead, being by itself. But someone may well say, "You have faith, and I have works; show me your faith without the works, and I will show you my faith by my works." You believe that God is one. You do well; the demons also believe, and shudder. But are you willing to recognize, you foolish fellow, that faith without works is useless?" James 2:17-20*

So when we know Jesus is Lord, how are we to respond? What is the effect of these words on us? How are we to react to such divine disclosure?

Perhaps like Paul long ago, after we queried, *"Who art Thou, Lord?" (Acts 9:5)* and He has shown us, we find ourselves crying out, *"What shall I do, Lord?"* (Acts 22:10). If so, we are in a good place. We are ready for the objective to be balanced with the subjective. We're ready for the Open Veil to be followed by the Open Heaven.

Sweet Lord,

May each of us be blessed as we pursue the heart of God. May each of us hear Your divine call and, whether it is fully understood or not, submit to it. May each of us so know Jesus that intellectual reality is commingled with relational activity. May each of us love Him more dearly as our Lord makes known to us the path of life. *"In Thy presence is fullness of joy; in Thy right hand there are pleasures forever."* (Psalm 16:11). We love You, Lord!

I shall walk before the LORD in the land of the living. Psalm 116:9

Chapter 12

What is Lordship?

The fear of the LORD is the beginning of wisdom; a good understanding have all those who do His commandments; His praise endures forever. Psalm 111:10

The knowledge that Jesus is Lord is not the end of the matter. Acknowledging His right to rule is a breakthrough, but it is only part of the gift. Declaring His supremacy is a beginning, but it is only half the blessing. While some may be on their knees in praise and thanksgiving that Jesus is the divinely appointed Lord, others with a somewhat less adoring and submissive attitude may be saying, in crude vernacular, "So what? Should I care? Even if He is, how could that affect me?"

In the human realm, many are entitled chief or leader or boss. Declared the leaders, they are authorized to govern certain aspects of other people's lives to gain a certain end. Within specific areas, according to predetermined parameters, with duties defined, they combine title and power to rule their sphere or domain.

For example, a boss or employer has the right to rule those who work for him in order to achieve his, not their, goals. A medical supervisor is in charge of nurses at certain times and patients in certain areas. Or, a school principal oversees and directs the activities of the teachers and students under his jurisdiction.

Too, in the specific realm of human government, a father is head of his own household, a chief leads his own tribe, and a pastor is given authority to spiritually oversee his own flock. Similarly, a king rules his kingdom and a lord commands his lordship.

Lordship then is exercising jurisdiction, sovereignty and rulership. It is leading or being master of areas where permission has specifically been granted to do so. It is exercising supremacy, extending rule, governing, guiding, and, if need be, enforcing a set way.

Yet lords and others who govern have one thing in common. No matter their arena or level of authority, no matter how high and public or how low and unknown, all human authorities are themselves under authority.

First of all, human authority is subject to higher human authority. Again using the earlier mentioned examples, a job boss or foreman is subject to the owners of the company that employs him. A medical floor superintendent is required to follow orders and oversee or enforce the policies of the medical facility he or she works for. A school principal is subordinate to and therefore accountable to the Superintendent of schools and the school board.

Too, in areas of government, fathers are subject to cultural, social, civil, and religious law in their stewardship of families and homes; the authority of tribal chiefs is related to the guiding principles of the people as a whole; and pastors in their caretaking and overseeing duties are themselves overseen by area, district or regional boards. Even those like the self employed, owners of small businesses, or presidents, kings, tyrants or dictators who seem to be independent or untouchably beyond the rule of others are subject to the law of the land.

In short, those in authority are subject to the ones who granted the authority. It is not their right to become a law unto themselves but rather to extend the policies of those who employed them, enforce the rules of those to whom they are subject, and to accomplish the goals using the methods and ways of those to whom they are in relationship.

Further, there is Another who is above all human leaders and sovereign over all human rulership. He is Jesus. No human being who was, is, or ever will be, no lord, from neophyte to the most aged and wise head of state, is separate from or independent of this higher Lord (Psalm 2). Whether a man or woman exercises authority without seeming to be under any other headship or whether he is obviously subject to the leadership of another on the human level, he is always subject to the Lordship of Another on the holy level. Ultimately, since God made Jesus Lord and all authority has been given to Him, any extension of authority to man which enables man to do His work is a gift from the Lord and subject to Him.

The Lordship of Jesus Christ then is supreme sovereignty. It is overall Mastery. Through it, He seeks to extend the kingdom of God on earth. He does so by overseeing the establishment, revelation, and enforcement of the law of the Lord. In His Lordship, there is no authority higher than His, no head wiser than His, no heart more loving than His. He is Lord of all!

Human and holy authority can be understood by a story in scripture. In Matthew 8:5-13, we learn of a Roman centurion. This man was an officer in the Roman army, head of a group of one hundred soldiers who served in the powerful military force that ruled and governed the world in the first century. Aware of his own position, the centurion said:

> *"For I, too, am a man under authority, with soldiers under me; and I say to this one, 'Go!' and he goes, and to another, 'Come!' and he comes, and to my slave, 'Do this!' and he does it." Matthew 8:9*

Yet when this high official, this captain of warriors, this ruler over the lives of others had a problem that was beyond his area of mastery, governance, or expertise, he recognized a much higher authority, Jesus, and sought His help. Honoring Him by coming to Him, addressing Him as Lord, he appealed to Him to exercise authority in a specific area of His holy Lordship. He entreated Him to heal his paralyzed servant.

Human authority bowed to holy authority. And with His heart of compassion, Jesus answered this expression of submission and faith. The Word declares the outcome.

> *And Jesus said to the centurion, "Go your way; let it be done to you as you have believed." And the servant was healed that very hour. Matthew 8:13*

The truth is that like the human rulers discussed earlier or the Roman centurion whose story was just told, each of us has been given an area or areas of authority. We have been raised and placed in a position to serve. And, while we may be lord over our specific domain and be extending lordship by the most honorable exercise of authority, we are still under the sovereignty of the Lord, Jesus Christ. Whether saint or sinner, believer or unbeliever, Christian or persecutor of Christians, whether we know it or not, like it or not, or acknowledge it or not, we are all under the authority of a higher Lord and must submit our sovereignty, leadership and governance to His higher rule. No matter the time, placement, or circumstances, we are all under the Lordship of the One whom God exalted and made Lord: Jesus Christ.

If we accept that Jesus is Lord and we submit to His Lordship, we must set all other questionable lordship aside. It means all personal attempts at lordship must be deposed. It means if any person or thing is illegally usurping Jesus' right to rule our lives or any situation is hindering our response to His Lordship, it must be rejected. Whether the challenge is from within or without, it must be met with fierce resistance.

While there surely are times (such as on the job or in proper family relationships) where it is good to yield to rightly established human authority, we cannot allow people or events to govern us in unholy ways. Our primary relationship and accountability is always with Jesus Christ, not man. In many ways and at many times all of us will be tempted or forcefully told to allow others to control our lives. Care must always be exercised to bow to legitimate authority but to reject the illegal.

First on the list of those illegally trying to dominate us by assaulting our decision to submit to holy Lordship is Satan. Until we are reborn, he has ruled our lives. With salvation, his authority is ended. He has been deposed, put down, thrown off the seat of government, and removed as ruler of our lives. Since he doesn't want us to know that and since he wants to reestablish illegal control over us, he will assault, badger, war with us and harass us while mocking or denying that Jesus is Lord and that Jesus rightfully rules over us.

Families are an area of concern, too. There are some situations where human authority is genuine and right for us. There are some instances where it is very wrong. Only prayer in the presence of God will discern which is which.

For instance, we are commanded to honor our father and our mother (Exodus 20:12). It is they who rightfully exercised parental authority over us, they who were to love, nourish, nurture, guide, protect and provide security for us when we were children. But if they are still exercising authority over us when we have grown into adulthood by trying to control our lives, families or jobs, or interfering with our marriages, that authority must be rejected. Likewise, husbands are to love their wives (Ephesians 5:28). But, if their leadership is abusive, it is an illegal representation of the Lordship of Jesus Christ and must be rejected.

A further example of family authority wrongfully exercised is the attempt of parents (or other relatives) to use their offspring to get their own unholy demands met, their own personal ambitions fulfilled, or to make them what they, not the Lord, want them to be. Their demands for security or prestige through their children may be stumbling blocks; their personal ambitions for them can lead them away from God's will for them. In His strength, these heirs can only reject this false authority and submit to the truth.

Perhaps the most familiar enemy hindering our relationship with the Lord is self. When we were reborn, it was not so we would set up a kingdom of self. No throne of self, no realm of self, no self rule, no self service is biblically or divinely acceptable. We were reborn to acknowledge that Jesus is Lord and to submit our self to His rule.

Agreeing that we do not have an independent existence and will never be separate from the sovereignty of God means lordship of self, lordship over our own life, lordship over our mind, emotions and will, lordship over our personal dreams, desires, ambitions, and goals, and lordship over our lordship of others must give place to the superior Lordship of Jesus Christ.

Even as we must set all interfering lordship aside, so in yielding to the Lordship of the One God exalted and made Lord, we must use Jesus as our example. Because we are told we will do greater works than Jesus did (John 14:12), because we too are to extend the Father's kingdom on earth, we must emulate Him. We must complete the desires of His heart, not ours, and exercise godly authority to fulfill our Father's and not our personal will. Like Moses and so many other giants of faith, we must see our lordship as an extension of His, a representation of Him, our earthly presentation of His heavenly sovereignty, and use it to fulfill His plan.

Jesus is the epitome of all things holy. The fruit of the Spirit is the expression of His heart. All that is good and great is in Him. He is the perfection of Lordship. His mastery is flawless; His rule is faultless. In our service to God, in fulfilling our part of the plan and will of God, can we do better than to follow the example of His preeminent leadership?

Can it be seen then that anything holding any saint back from service in areas of divinely appointed leadership (or lordship) is an attempt to hinder the government of God? Can we see that anytime we yield to such intrusion, we sin against the sovereignty of God? Whatever holds us back from true obedience, interferes with our walk, clouds us with confusion, or fills us with carnal warfare or inner conflict indicates that our relationship with our Lord is under assault and submission to His Lordship is incomplete.

The realm of authority of Jesus Christ far surpasses any other known throughout the course of human history. The scope of the places, times, and areas over which He has dominion is not known to man. His Lordship is so all encompassing, whole, complete and perfect that it is impossible to bring it down to man's level for comparison.

Jesus' rule has no limits. He is Lord of all. Therefore He has dominion over all. He is Ruler of all, living and dead. He is sovereign over all, the One with the right to exercise divine authority in every place at any time. Nothing is beyond His ability. There is nowhere that His arm is not allowed to reach or His voice not permitted to speak. There is no one excused from responding to His presence and sovereignty by instant and complete obedience.

The Lordship of Jesus Christ is His right to rule in His Father's place. It is His legitimate exercise of authority of the kingdom of God over the kings, both secular and spiritual, of God. It is His rulership over earth and over us. We are privileged to bow to Him.

But Jesus called them to Himself, and said, "You know that the rulers of the Gentiles lord it over them, and their great men exercise authority over them. It is not so among you, but whoever wishes to become great among you shall be your servant, and whoever wishes to be first among you shall be your slave; just as the Son of Man did not come to be served, but to serve, and to give His life a ransom for many." Matthew 20: 25-28

Chapter 13

Jesus at the Jordan

"THE VOICE OF ONE CRYING IN THE WILDERNESS, 'MAKE READY THE WAY OF THE LORD, MAKE HIS PATHS STRAIGHT!'" Matthew 3:4

Salvation is the defining moment in every Christian's life. It is that singular and momentous occasion in which each of us must acknowledge and confess our sins and ask Jesus to save us from them. Then, by the power of His once shed blood, our sins are forgiven. Through the miracles of His death, burial, and resurrection, we are reborn from above. His Holy Spirit 1) quickens our spirits to new life in Christ; and 2) He comes to dwell in each saint. In essence, we have asked Jesus to be our Savior and He has responded with wonderful expressions of love and blessing.

While salvation is the singular requirement of all who want to spend eternity with Jesus, it is NOT His only expression of favor. Though spiritual rebirth brings us into our holy heritage and makes us aware of His promises to us, it is but the fount of grace from which other blessings flow as we work out our salvation with fear and trembling in the Lord.

There is another special moment that stands out in the lives of many Christians. It is that time when we acknowledge that we cannot live without His help, choose not to be in control of our own lives (or the lives of those around us), and ask Jesus to govern us instead. By the power of the Spirit

He sends to us, we surrender to God; by the love of the Spirit who fills us, we yield more and more control until our lives become His. In essence, we have asked Jesus to be our Lord.

A little background information is helpful. Though we are living in this world, we are not of this natural world. Once born again, we are of the kingdom of God. The kingdom of God is not natural but supernatural. For a Christian to live a supernatural life in a supernatural kingdom, supernatural provision is required.

In the world, human authority is often a matter of who can be made subservient to whom or who can dominate and control whom. However, in the kingdom of God, authority is related to servanthood. True spiritual authority comes as a result of the desire to serve rather than to be served. It is the fruit of yielding worldly authority, giving up areas of control, letting go of the rope, and becoming a servant of God.

For example, Moses was given supernatural authority after he gave up life in Pharaoh's court where he could demand the highest level of service that the world could offer, after he gave up areas of personal control where he could do anything he wanted to do no matter what the effect was on others, and after he gave up the seclusion and protection of life in the desert to serve God.

To walk in spiritual authority, each saint must be able to discern between human and holy or between soul and spirit. Soul is our inner man, a combination of intellect, emotion, and will which makes up and includes our nature, personality, and essential being. Our spirit is our innermost man, quickened to life at salvation. Separate from either body or soul, it is our immaterial, invisible being which enjoys and reflects the life of God within.

Before salvation, our souls were enthroned, governing our minds and bodies by worldly standards and ruling by personal whim. As part of a natural rather than supernatural being, soul was concerned with self. It's rule aggrandized self: self determination using self will to bring self effort to pass;

self gratification and self indulgence for self pleasure; self governing for self promotion; self defense, self justification and self preservation when things look bad; self pity, self assertiveness, and self esteem to make them look good again. The list goes on.

But salvation changes all of that. Soul and self are no longer in charge. They are not to continue ruling as they once did. God quickens the highest part of our beings, our spirits, to new life. Our reborn spirits are in communion with the Spirit of God and are governed by His voice. Spirit dethrones the god of self and leads us to submit to the God of glory (Psalm 29:3). Holy Spirit challenges our human spirits to serve the God of our salvation (1 Chronicles 16:35).

There is usually a difficult internal struggle as the war goes on wherein soul and self are continually called on to yield more of their control to God's Spirit. But as we saints persist, as we are doggedly determined to make a successful transition from self serving to servant to God, our spirits rise and take their ordained places. As we walk in the spirit, as we yield control to the Holy Spirit, we become spiritual beings. As we grow in spirit and are led by the Spirit, we focus less on self and more on the Lord. As we center on Him, we learn with deepening joy that He reigns over all; every human, natural, carnal, worldly kingdom of man whether financial, commercial, medical, educational, artistic, or religious, is subject to Him and His will and purposes. And as we seek Him, we understand that our salvations were not just for our sakes but for His. We were saved to be--and saved to do. We were saved or brought into right relationship with God to be like Jesus, growing in the fruit of the Spirit who indwells us. And, we were saved to do the works of God as Jesus did through the gifts of His Spirit who infills us.

To relate all of this to the Lordship of Jesus Christ, we must go to the Jordan River. As written in the gospels of Matthew and Luke, Jesus came to the Jordan to be baptized. The significance of His action goes far beyond the obvious, and understanding it may cause us to be less quick to quench the Holy Spirit in our lives.

To put the story in context, John the Baptist had been preaching a message of repentance in the Judean wilderness. Part of his announcement revealed his urgency.

"Repent, for the kingdom of heaven is at hand." Matthew 3:2

A second part of his message revealed how to respond to this word.

"MAKE READY THE WAY OF THE LORD, MAKE HIS PATHS STRAIGHT!" Matthew 3:3

And a third part of the message more fully described this LORD whose way was to be made ready.

"As for me, I baptize you with water for repentance, but He who is coming after me is mightier than I, and I am not fit to remove His sandals; He will baptize you with the Holy Spirit and fire. Matthew 3:11

John the Baptist was a mighty man of God who declared the need for repentance and who baptized in water those who responded to him by confessing their sins. Yet, he was fully aware that a mightier Man of God was coming who would baptize them in the Holy Spirit.

While John refers to preparing the way of the LORD, the Bible clearly identifies this LORD as Jesus.

"Then Jesus arrived from Galilee at the Jordan coming to John, to be baptized by him." Matthew 3:13

At first, John was upset and tried to prevent Jesus from submitting Himself to him for baptism (verse 14). After all, Jesus who had no sin had no need to be forgiven of sin. Yet Jesus overruled John and yielded Himself for immersion in water saying:

"Permit it at this time; for in this way it is fitting for us to fulfill all righteousness." (verse 15).

But that wasn't the end of it. Of the many from Jerusalem, Judea, and the area around the Jordan who had previously been baptized by John, the Bible records no unusual events. But when Jesus had been baptized in water to fulfill all righteousness, even as He arose from the healing, cleansing waters, the supernatural broke forth. That we recall what happened and begin to understand its full impact, the event is here quoted from the gospels of both Matthew and Luke.

> *And after being baptized, Jesus went up immediately from the water; and behold, the heavens were opened, and he saw the Spirit of God descending as a dove, and coming upon Him, and behold, a voice out of the heavens, saying, "This is My beloved Son, in whom I am well-pleased." Matthew 3:16,17*

> *Now it came about when all the people were baptized, that Jesus also was baptized, and while He was praying, heaven was opened, and the Holy Spirit descended upon Him in bodily form like a dove, and a voice came out of heaven, "Thou art My beloved Son, in Thee I am well-pleased." Luke 3:21,22*

The first thing to note is that Father, Son, and Holy Spirit all take part in this planned and holy wonder. This event was not by chance; it was ordained by the will of the whole Godhead.

As soon as Jesus went up from the water, He had an extraordinary visitation. The heavens were opened. Skies that had been closed were opened so that something could be released. A man, John, who usually couldn't see such things, saw the Spirit of God. This Spirit descended in bodily form as a dove and rested on Jesus. Surely some might wonder if the dove, not heard of since it was released from Noah's Ark to find a resting place, had now found it on Jesus.

And a man, John, who usually couldn't hear such things, heard the voice of God who identified Jesus as His cherished Son and pronounced His delight in Him. In Matthew's version, God addressed man and presents Jesus. In Luke's account, God speaks to Jesus and identifies and affirms Him.

What had just happened? Jesus had come from Galilee to the Jordan to John to be baptized. This was a special place for a special purpose for a special Man. Immediately after He stepped into the river, was immersed, and came up out of the water, the Holy Spirit came on Him. Then in a supernatural way, Jesus received the anointing or empowerment to do the works God had sent Him to do. John had called Him Lord. The Holy Spirit was initiating His Lordship. By the sign of the dove descending and resting on Him, the Holy Spirit was confirming that Jesus and no other was that Lord, and that Jesus and no other had been given holy power to carry out this Lordship.

As we know, in the Bible, the Lord is identified as the Spirit. "*Now the Lord is the Spirit,*" (2 Corinthians 3:17). The same verse goes on to declare that the Lord has a Spirit. "*...and where the Spirit of the Lord is, there is liberty.*"

In this last phrase, the words "of the" declare possession. For instance, when scripture speaks about the feasts of the Lord (Leviticus 23:2), He owns or has proprietorship of them. When it talks of the law of the Lord (Psalm 119:1), or the congregation of the Lord (Numbers 27:17), He established them and possesses them. And surely, the name of the Lord belongs to Him. It is His and no other can have it.

In like manner, the Spirit of the Lord is the Lord's Spirit. It belongs to Him. It is His alone. When the Holy Spirit descended on the Lord, whose way John had prepared, He became the Spirit of that Lord. Since Jesus is that prophesied Lord and the One on whom the Spirit rested, Jesus owns, has, or possesses the Spirit of the Lord. The Spirit of the Lord is His.

This extraordinary event at the Jordan happened for one reason: to enable Jesus to act as Lord or to anoint Him into His Lordship; to empower Him to be a Servant, and from that position to be Leader, Ruler, Master, and Sovereign, all by the power of the Holy, not human, Spirit. The Holy Spirit came on the Lord Jesus so He could express God's will, introduce His government, be His representative, and extend His kingdom by holy anointing.

In this ministry, Jesus would be wholly subject to God by the Spirit of God. He would give up self to yield to the heart, desires, plan, purposes, and will of God as revealed by the Spirit of God. He would surrender all control of His life, setting aside personal thoughts, feelings, and choices, and give His Father first place in all He said and did. Under the anointing of Lordship, He would allow the Holy Spirit to infill Him, possess Him, and direct Him as He willingly submitted to His guidance and manifested His power. Only from such a place of anointed surrender could Jesus later say concerning His sacrifice for our salvation: *"My Father, if it is possible, let this cup pass from Me: yet not as I will, but as Thou wilt."* (Matthew 26:39).

Jesus' Open Heaven affects all of our lives. His experience at the Jordan is recorded as our example. It is the Father's desire that the Holy Spirit indwell each saint. And it is the Father's desire that heaven opens and the Holy Spirit comes to rest on each saint to empower each saint.

In our Christian walk, we come to a place where we understand that if Jesus said He did nothing on His own initiative (John 8:28), neither should we; or when He said He did not seek His own will (John 5:30), neither can we. And when He said, *"...for I have come down from heaven not to do My own will, but the will of Him who sent Me."* (John 6:38), so must we.

While the Spirit is the Lord's, Jesus is eager to share Him. God wants each saint to take part in the kingdom of God. He wants us to continue our Lord's work. While it was the Father who sent the Holy Spirit to Jesus, it is now Jesus in heaven who baptizes us in the Holy Spirit. When we acknowledge that apart from Him we can do nothing (John 15:5) and seek Him as our strength, Jesus does not physically return to rest on us and anoint us into His works. He sends His Spirit upon us.

This does not mean that we all have to make a pilgrimage to the Jordan to legalistically emulate Jesus' experience. He will meet us where we are. John cried out to prepare the way of the Lord and when His way was made ready, Jesus came and was anointed by the Spirit. Just so, we need to cry out, to prepare the way of the Lord toward us, and then wait to see how He moves in our lives to orchestrate the descent of His Spirit upon us. As our salvations were personal and tailored to our particular lives and circumstances, so too our baptism into His Spirit will be specific to us. Jesus was a special Man who God met at a special time and place in a very special way to do a most special work. From God's point of view, so are we.

To receive His Spirit, we must do several things. First, we must die to self. The Jordan River is symbolic of death to self. We must willingly, even eagerly, come to our Jordan, refuse the mantle of the old carnal man and walk in and be led by the Holy Spirit even as we continuously yield control of our lives to the Lord of our lives.

Second, we must agree to do God's will with the measure of anointing given us. As we mature in the power of the Holy Spirit, we need to understand that He has not rested on us for any expression of self ambition, self indulgence or self aggrandizement. He is there solely that we may do God's will in His time and in His way. Any less is disobedience; any more is presumption.

Third, we must realize that we can only do God's will through the power of God's Spirit. No counterfeit source of ability, enablement, or empowerment is acceptable.

If at any point of our ministry unto God we find ourselves struggling with the issue of the preeminence of God, tired of being in second place to Him, or clashing with Him in ideas, judgments, values, or morals, offended when self is thwarted, greedy for power but indifferent about the Source of the power, or finding it hard to decrease so that He may increase, we need to go back to our Jordan. We haven't truly died to self.

If we won't wait on the Lord until we know His will for our anointing, if we are angry that He is shrinking our boundaries or pulling us out of ministries which we may enjoy or to which He never called us, if we realize we have become susceptible to flattery and manipulation because of the power on us, if we want to use God's Spirit to fulfill our dreams, or if we want personal fame and renown in the use of particular gifts, we need to go back to our Jordan. We haven't fully surrendered to God's will.

If we still believe we are wise enough to lead others or strong enough to extend the kingdom of God without the power of God, if we are placing people above God, using people or being used by them, if we are not willing or able to differentiate the Holy Spirit from another spirit and are therefore dabbling in the occult as an alternative source of power, we need to go back to our Jordan. We haven't sanctified the Holy Spirit as the only fountain of holy anointing.

At our Jordan we need to repent, humble ourselves and seek God. When we are in right relationship with Him, we can ask for a refilling of His precious Spirit. What greater joy could we have when like Jesus, the Holy Spirit comes to rest on us, our Father identifies us as His son or daughter, and He declares His delight and pleasure in us?

Praise the LORD! How blessed is the man who fears the LORD, who greatly delights in His commandments. Psalm 112:1

୧୦

Chapter 14

Jesus Undergoing Temptation

Then Jesus was led up by the Spirit into the wilderness to be tempted by the devil. Matthew 4:1

When Scripture was first written, it was not divided up into numbered verses and chapters as it is now. These additions came later when translators attempted to introduce a universal means of order and clarity to the various books. While such divisions do help our reading and researching, they sometimes hinder our understanding. Often we are not aware that certain portions of scripture are meant to be connected, one a progression of another. While isolated incidents and stories do instruct and inspire us, it is only when they are kept in context and viewed together with the verses that surround them that we can see the greater perspective and learn the broader lessons.

Such is the case with the scriptures we are studying about Jesus. His coming to the Jordan was part of a series of events, each valuable for instruction and application to life in its own right, but all of which are needed to complete the canvas God is painting. These events are:

• John the Baptist preaching in the wilderness, exhorting people to prepare the way of the Lord.

- Jesus fulfilling John's prophecy that the kingdom of God was at hand by appearing at the Jordan.

- Jesus' insistence on water baptism.

- The Holy Spirit coming to rest on Him.

- The Holy Spirit leading Jesus to the wilderness to be tempted.

- Jesus' return to Nazareth.

- Jesus' entry into His earthly ministry.

The first four of these were covered in the last chapter. The last two will be dealt with in Chapter 14. In this chapter, discussion will center on the fifth point: Jesus' temptations.

Immediately after the heavens opened, Jesus was presented with the opportunity to obey the Spirit who had descended to rest on Him. He was called upon to follow the Spirit out into the wilderness.

The idea of this wilderness trek did not originate with the Lord. He had just been highly exalted, given honor, and spiritually provisioned for the work ahead. He could have resisted the directive to the desert in a desire to begin His ministry and miracles. He could have refused to take a time-consuming detour in order to get on with His own agenda. But Jesus knew that though He had authority, He must remain under authority. Instead of demanding His own way or pursuing any personal plans, He chose obedience. He submitted to the will of the Spirit and was led into the wilderness.

When Mark records this event in his gospel, he uses a much more powerful verb for the word "led" than either Matthew or Luke did. When he says, "… *immediately the Spirit impelled Him to go out into the wilderness…*', (Mark 1:12), he meant that Jesus was driven out, pushed out or cast out. Jesus was not joyfully led away to the desert; He was thrust into it.

The purpose of the desert trek was testing and trial by the enemy of all men.

Then Jesus was led up by the Spirit into the wilderness to be tempted by the devil. (Matthew 4:1)

Throughout scripture (and in life), it is apparent that some tests men face are for their good. They are designed to prove the worth of a man, to show him areas of victory he has gained, or to reveal his strength in Christ. These come from God. Other trials are designed to do just the opposite. They are to entice a man to do evil, to reveal the baseness of his character, to manipulate him into doing things which are contrary to the will of God, and then to leave him in a state of despair about ever rising from the filth and mire. These come from the devil.

Though it was the Spirit who led Jesus into the desert, His trials were from the prince of tempters. The tests were to solicit the Son of God to commit sin. They were an attempt to draw Jesus into evil so the spotless Lamb would be unfit as a perfect sacrifice. They were an appeal to Jesus to act as a carnal, natural man so concerned with self that He would excuse Himself from His part in God's plan of salvation and thus thwart the will of God.

In these particular temptations God, who was in charge, allowed the tests to show why He was so proud of and pleased with His Son; His enemy hoped through the trials to prove this Father's blessings misplaced. He wanted to destroy Jesus' character which would annul His calling.

To some, a desert is a delightfully remote area that provides a place of solitude, peace, and reflection when life is overwhelming. Others see the desert as a challenge, a place to live while confronting and gaining victory over forces that could destroy them. To many, and surely that includes most Christians, deserts are hot, barren, painful places of testing and trials.

In fact, a desert is a, '...*great and terrible wilderness, with its fiery serpents and scorpions and thirsty ground where there was no water.*" (Deuteronomy 8:15).

A desert is scorching hot during the day and freezing cold at night. It is seemingly barren and unfruitful, teeming with animals whose teeth can tear and pests whose tails can sting. Lacking food, deprived of water, and without companionship, to the unaware the desert is not a friendly place to be.

And yet, powerful anointing notwithstanding, the Holy Spirit's first directive to Jesus was to go into the desert. Jesus was thrust into an area where His comfort zones were removed, where there were no amenities to ease the extremes of nature, and where defense and protection became matters of faith in God. After fasting for forty days and nights in such conditions, He had a visitor. When He was physically weakened, the tempter came.

Suddenly the desert became an arena. Two duelers raised their weapons. The battle was on!

In the premier clash, the devil thrust at Jesus about His identification. His words, *"If You are the Son of God…"* (Matthew 4:3) must have sounded like the slash of a murderous blade hissed out at his opponent.

All who had been at the Jordan could testify that God had declared Jesus to be His Son. Yet even in this seemingly settled point of strength, the enemy tried to introduce doubt. His opening thrust was to cause Jesus to question His relationship with His father and, because of His present debilitated condition, to make His Father seem like an uncaring, unloving, unconcerned parent.

The second part of this initial trial challenged Jesus to decide in which kingdom, the world or heaven, He would operate. If He was a human son of a man, He could possibly be persuaded to use His supernatural anointing in carnal ways; if He was the holy Son of God, He would wait to use them for spiritual reasons by the order of God.

Asking Jesus to miraculously provide food for His hungry flesh was merely a feint. The devil's real intent was to incite Jesus, weakened as He was, to use His power in a way He was not authorized. Specifically, the temptation was to use spiritual power for human gratification. And that the devil wanted

Jesus to cast aside the leadership of the Holy Spirit and yield to the control of his evil spirit is revealed in his words to Jesus, which are a command, not a suggestion.

"If You are the Son of God, command that these stones become bread." Matthew 4:3

Perhaps the enemy didn't know that Jesus had a weapon, too. In fact, His was a special spiritual sword. Since He is Lord, His weapon was a Lordly one: the sword of the Spirit. This sword was the word of God, armament which Jesus was able to use very effectively. He instantly won victory over this temptation with a word from scripture. Parrying with a deadly thrust from the book of Deuteronomy, He declared in essence that neither bread nor the personal use of spiritual gifts was the real issue. The Word of God was.

But He answered and said, "It is written, 'MAN SHALL NOT LIVE ON BREAD ALONE, BUT ON EVERY WORD THAT PRO-CEEDS OUT OF THE MOUTH OF GOD.'" Matthew 4:4

It is interesting that in His warfare, Jesus quoted from the book of Deuteronomy. This was the book that was always read before the armies of Israel went into battle. In the desert for forty days, communing with God, praying to the Father, it is possible He was given these very words with which to defeat the foe. Each time the devil attacked and Jesus used this weapon, He won the encounter. The words, "It is written" followed by the words of God were all that were needed.

In the second confrontation, the devil led Jesus into Jerusalem to the temple area. Oh! the effrontery that the adversary of all that is holy would dare tread in Jerusalem's holy city and his malignant presence blacken the sanctity of the holy temple.

Again the gauntlet was thrown down. This second contest also concerned presumption. It too was an attempt to get Jesus to use His supernatural powers to do things outside the will of God or to fulfill personal whim. On the pinnacle of the temple, the devil who had been defeated by Scripture now used Scripture to dare Jesus. Yielding no place to honor, fear, awe, respect, or submission to the divinity of God, he commanded:

> *"If You are the Son of God throw Yourself down; for it is written, 'HE WILL GIVE HIS ANGELS CHARGE CONCERNING YOU;' and 'ON their HANDS THEY WILL BEAR YOU UP, LEST YOU STRIKE YOUR FOOT AGAINST A STONE.'"* Matthew 4:6

For all who honor the devil by professing that he knows and quotes more scripture than Christians do, let it clearly be seen that he quotes what he wants to, leaves out what he wants to, and does so to gain his own evil ends. Here he partially quoted from Psalm 91, leaving out the important phrase *"...to guard you in all your ways."* (verse 11). God will guard and protect men when their ways are submitted to Him and under His blessing; but He has no obligation to men when they act foolishly, challenge the laws of nature in defiance of human physical or mental restrictions, and then expect Him to save them.

Again resisting the tempter's command to act improperly, Jesus quickly responded. Again His sword landed telling blows.

> *Jesus said to him, "On the other hand, it is written, 'YOU SHALL NOT PUT THE LORD YOUR GOD TO THE TEST.'"* Matthew 4:7.

In a few short words, Jesus attacked the devil's dismal attempt to confuse, misquote, and misuse scripture. First, His words revealed that the Lord was not required to respond to either willfully wrong, ignorant or misunderstood Scripture or to the deliberate attempt to use God's word to force God to act in certain ways. Then, He thrust home the point that the devil should not be tempting the Lord who was his God. Finally, He inflicted an almost mortal wound when He subtly identified Himself as the Lord who was that God. Even this devil had a God, One who was in authority and control over him and therefore One whom he should not be testing and trying.

Refusing to yield or admit defeat, the tempter then moved to the third and final confrontation. Since he now knew Jesus would not use the Holy Spirit who rested on Him for personal gain or in a presumptuous way, he sought to get Him to compromise. As viewed from a high mountain, he claimed to own all the kingdoms of the world and that they were available for a price. Jesus could have them if He would worship the devil. In complete defiance of the God he had once served, he introduced the epitome of false religion—the worship of a false god.

The bribery did not work. These kingdoms already belonged to Jesus and He would not accept them in that way. Without pause to even think the offer over, without hesitation, without debate, without analysis, without a moment to fantasize about the possibilities, without discussion, Jesus used His sword to slash the offer into pieces. For the first time, Jesus identified the tempter as Satan. For the first time He is the One to issue the command. Declaring that the offer was not an option, saying He didn't want premature authority over the world at that price, He refused His adversary.

Then Jesus said to him, "Begone, Satan! For it is written, 'YOU SHALL WORSHIP THE LORD YOUR GOD, AND SERVE HIM ONLY.'" Matthew 4:10

With this final victory, the duel was over. There was one Champion and one defeated foe. Baffled, confounded, unable to win, Satan retreated in disgrace. Bold, honorable, victorious, Jesus received ministry from angels.

If Jesus had an Open Heaven experience in which the Holy Spirit came to rest on Him and that same Spirit led Him away to be tested concerning that anointing, so will we be. None is exempt. As in all things, Jesus is our holy representative, our divine example. His temptations are a revelation of those we will face when the Holy Spirit has come to rest on, anoint, and empower us.

We should all understand that when we have received the blessing of God and fully intend to honor God with it by obediently using His power to do

His will, we become targets. It is the enemy's avowed purpose to stop us from doing so. If he can attack us when we are young and inexperienced, knock us out of the blocks at the very beginning of our assignments, come against us with unholy power at the start of our race and cause us to turn back, give up or shut down the anointing before we've really begun, he has gained his objective.

But, if we understand that we are led into or thrust into such painful challenges by that same Spirit, we can endure through them and find victory over them. We have to expect that the enemy of our souls will test us by trying to confuse us or make us doubt our identification and relationship with our Father. He will tempt us to sin against God by using our anointing in the Holy Spirit for personal gain, in presumptuous whim, or, in the ultimate evil, to obey the commands of Satan. If all this fails, he will try to force us to compromise our God.

The good news is that just as surely we can expect that God will allow this testing, each of us will have the opportunity to find inner strength in the power of His might and to emerge from the contest as more than a conqueror in Christ Jesus.

In earthly warfare, a weapon is a soldier's best friend. In like manner, in spiritual warfare, our weapon is our best friend. It is the same weapon that Jesus used so effectively: God's word. Often it is the only thing that gets us out of trouble. Sometimes it is the only thing that stands between us and death. Like soldiers who have fought in world wars, we who are enlisted in God's army must live with our weapon, eat with it, sleep with it, care for it, be completely familiar with it and never hesitate to use it as our only means of victory. If we want to survive the war, we must pick up our sword and slash Satan with it; that is we must announce, pronounce, declare and proclaim the Word of God.

Like Jesus, our tests may come in a variety of places. Our desert of testing may be a wilderness experience or the horror of the dark night of the soul.

It may be the isolation of a jail cell or the aftermath of the death of a loved one. But in it, we can learn who we are and enjoy a growing dependence on God. We can gain victory over the all too human tendency to see a need and fill it rather than see a need and wait on God.

Or, our pinnacle of trial may be the more open, widespread or even universal challenge of the public arena. It may be we have risen (or are rising) to the top of the ladder in our area of expertise and, though gaining name, reputation and position in the process, we want to be even more well known. It may be that we are comfortable with our lifestyle and fear losing it through illness, financial loss, or the call of God on our lives. It may be that from our lofty place we feel we are above it all, impervious to danger, and beyond the authority of men. But here we can learn not to cast aside care or take unnecessary and unwise chances or to jump into things without His sanction to do so. It is here we can learn that we are never above God and that He is not required to honor what He has not ordained.

Our high place of temptation may be God testing us to see if the desires of our hearts are the desires of His heart for us (Psalm 37: 4). It may be the chance to have whatever we want in the world--at a price. But even here, whenever we can see all things under our feet and know the unattainable can now be ours (like a coveted job, a house, a fiancé, power, financial security), we can learn to ask who is offering our dream to us and why. And we can learn that if we receive the wrong answers to the questions, we cannot compromise. Nothing comes without a price and God is not for sale.

Being in the Spirit and being in the wilderness seems to be a contradiction. But if led by the Spirit to be in the wilderness, it is not. It is only by overcoming the tests and trials that He leads us to and through that we can conquer the wilderness, and only after we have gained a measure of character that God can trust us with His holy power.

The truth is, that after the Open Heaven experience, after the coming of the Holy Spirit upon us in power, the time in the desert is a great blessing. God ordained the experience for Jesus. So He does with us. God allowed Jesus to be tempted. So He does with us. Jesus defeated the enemy with His sword. So can we. Jesus is the Champion. So are we—in Him.

Yet the Lord is faithful, and He will strengthen [you] and set you on a firm foundation and guard you from the evil [one]. 2 Thessalonians 3:3 (AMP)

Chapter 15

Jesus at Nazareth

Blessed is the one who comes in the name of the LORD; Psalm 118:26

Having established Himself over Satan and his devilish realm, it was now time for Jesus to reveal Himself to mankind. And, having been identified as the Son of God to a few, it was now time to present His credentials of Lordship and power to many. It was the season for Jesus to move beyond manifesting His Father's nature only; He was now to manifest His power, too. So that people would stop looking for the Lord and realize He was already among them, it was the hour for Jesus to do both: be like His Father and to do His Father's will.

Scripture has described the Open Heaven event where the Holy Spirit came upon Jesus at the Jordan River. It has also detailed the trials wherein Jesus put His enemy on notice that He, not Satan, was Lord and that He, not Satan, would accomplish His Father's will through His Father's Spirit. But both of these events are incomplete without the next several verses of scripture. Jesus' anointing and His trials are misunderstood without the revelation of what He was to do with His blessing.

It was time for Jesus to move from defense to offense—to get about His Father's business. Detailing the last of the remarkable trio of events, the word announces the beginning of Jesus' public ministry.

Surely it is right that the formal proclamation of the service of the anointed and victorious Jesus should be among those who knew Him: family, friends, neighbors and those who ate at tables He built or worked with carts and tools He mended. Surely it is fitting that the quotation from scripture describing and declaring His ministry should be read where it had first been learned. Appropriately, Jesus returned to His hometown of Nazareth, "… *and as was His custom, He entered the synagogue on the Sabbath and stood up to read" (Luke 4:16).*

And the book of the prophet Isaiah was handed to Him. And He opened the book, and found the place where it was written,

> *"THE SPIRIT OF THE LORD IS UPON ME, BECAUSE HE ANOINTED ME TO PREACH THE GOSPEL TO THE POOR. HE HAS SENT ME TO PROCLAIM RELEASE TO THE CAP-TIVES, AND RECOVERY OF SIGHT TO THE BLIND, TO SET FREE THOSE WHO ARE DOWNTRODDEN, TO PROCLAIM THE FAVORABLE YEAR OF THE LORD." Luke 4:17-19*

In a few short words, Jesus encompassed His future. First, in this extraordinary announcement, He gave His qualification for service: *"The Spirit of the LORD is upon Me…".*

The only way Jesus could do all that His Father wanted Him to do was by the Spirit or essence or power of God upon Him. Here, the Father's Spirit had superimposed Himself, come over, or impressed or imprinted Himself on the Father's Son. And this Spirit was His eligibility, His prerequisite, His skill, talent or ability, His enablement to serve.

Second, Jesus spoke of His commissioning: *"He anointed Me…".*

Sending the Spirit on Jesus was a sovereign choice and act of God. Jesus didn't do it. No other human did it. No other power did it. God and God alone had done it.

Third, the Spirit had been sent and Jesus was anointed for a specific calling: *"...He anointed Me to..."*.

It could not be more definite that the Spirit or empowerment of God was to accomplish certain things. So certain was Jesus of His mission that He publicly detailed it. He revealed the multitude of responsibility given Him to be accomplished by the Spirit on Him.

In the power of the Spirit, Jesus was to:

- Preach the gospel or proclaim the good news to the poor which would include the financially strapped as well as the poor in things of God

- Deliver those bound, freeing them from the kingdom of darkness and/or bring release to those bedeviled by unholy spirits who were in the kingdom of God

- Heal, cure, or make whole those suffering from infirmity, disease, weakness, and, in some cases, even death

- Heal or restore the down trodden, bruised, wounded, desperate, desolate, forsaken, rejected, and abused

- Declare the acceptable year of the Lord.

Those hearing and believing those words must have been astonished. For long ages and generations until John the Baptist arrived, the voice of the prophets had not been heard. In the centuries of time between Malachi and Matthew, there is no biblical record of the power of God moving among men. In this time, holy light had darkened. Hope had turned to despair. But now Jesus spoke words of glory to those long bound in death, disability, sickness, and sin. He was announcing a ministry of the miraculous that would return the presence and power of God to men.

Participation in this miraculous blessing was contingent upon acknowledging two truths. First, when Jesus said, *"The Spirit of the Lord is on Me..."*, He was announcing that the Holy Spirit or empowerment by God's Spirit was the Father's only ordained way to accomplish His goals or do His will. The power of God's Spirit was the only legitimate way by which these blessings would be manifested. Nothing would be done by Jesus the Man. Nothing could be done by human might, strength, power or striving. Nothing should be done by the invocation or acceptance of demonic power. The Father had sent His Spirit on Jesus. Jesus was Lord. The Spirit of the Lord would, could, and should do these things.

Second, when Jesus said, "*The Spirit of the Lord is on Me...*", He was declaring He was Ruler or Leader. His strong and uncompromising words rendered null and void any challenge that God's ministry to men could come through any other person. Since the Spirit was on Him, any who wanted the blessings of salvation, healing, deliverance, and victory had to get them through Him.

Jesus was really saying, "The passage from Isaiah I am about to quote is My area of ministry. Its works fall under My area of rulership or expertise. I am Head or Chief or Lord over them all. I am the One who has been given authority to represent My Father about them and the One empowered to accomplish His will concerning them." Since all of those in the synagogue (and every man, woman, and child who has lived from then to now) was in some way affected by or in need of ministry in at least one of the areas of His sovereignty, Jesus was giving all who heard Him the option of coming under the umbrella of His Lordship. Jesus was Lord of all!

After Jesus' proclamation that memorable Sabbath, He did as charged to do. The generic statement of ministry was followed by specific acts which fulfilled His Father's plan. He called men to repentance (Matthew 4:17), preached, taught, healed and delivered (verses 23,24). And in all He did, His words and acts of power never missed a chance to glorify His Father and draw men unto Him.

With all of this in mind, perhaps we, as the early disciples did, can better understand the use of the word Lord in our scriptures. For example, when the disciples wanted to know how to pray, they called on the Lord who taught them to evangelize or call down the kingdom of God (Luke 11:1). When the leper asked to be healed, he appealed to Jesus as Lord, not as Lamb or Lion (Luke 5:12). Or, we can sense the astonishment of the Pharisees when Jesus annulled their control over legalistic forms of religion by declaring Himself to be Lord, Ruler, Master of the Sabbath (Mark 2:28). In all of these areas, praying, healing or releasing the captives, Jesus, the Lord, had been given the right to rule in the lives of men so it was more than appropriate that those men call upon Him as Lord for help.

As heaven opened for Jesus so that the Holy spirit might descend on Him to anoint Him for service, so it will be opened for us that our Father's Spirit might come to rest upon us for our service unto Him. As Jesus underwent a series of tests designed by the enemy to hinder and halt God's purposes for the anointing, so too we will face trials meant to harass and hinder, to cause us to give up, to harm or even kill us to stop the fulfillment of God's will through us by His Spirit.

And as there was a time and way by which Jesus began His public ministry, so God has a plan for making ours known. As Jesus was aware of the aim of His anointing, announced it, and then set about doing it, so we, through communion with God, come to know His purpose in empowering us and must set about doing it. Like Jesus, it is often revealed in general terms and then worked out in specific details at specific times involving specific circumstances, places, and people as the Holy Spirit directs. And to many who are lost in the world or worn out in the church, the anointing to speak, heal, release, and revive will be received as manna from heaven.

If we are to enjoy a successful ministry, there are several truths we must always honor. First, moving under the anointing of the Holy Spirit is still the only way to accomplish God's will. When Jesus was on earth, He ministered by the Spirit of God. Before He ascended to His Father in heaven, He acknowledged His work on earth was not finished (John 14:12). Indicating that others, His disciples, the church, or saints of God, were to complete it, He specifically detailed what would need to be done to finish it. Sounding remarkably like the passage in Luke 4, these tasks included:

> " *Go therefore and make disciples of all the nations, baptizing them in the name of the Father and the Son and the Holy Spirit, teaching them to observe all that I commanded you; and lo, I am with you always, even to the end of the age." Matthew 28:19,20*

> *"Go into all the world and preach the gospel to all creation. He who has believed and has been baptized shall be saved; but he who has disbelieved shall be condemned. And these signs will accompany those who have believed: in My name they will cast out demons, they will speak with new tongues; they will pick up serpents, and if they drink any deadly poison, it shall not hurt them; they will lay hands on the sick, and they will recover." Mark 16:15-18*

Jesus not only told His followers what they were to do; He also stated how they were to do it. His disciples were to stay in Jerusalem, *"to wait for what the Father had promised"* (Acts 1:4). This promise was the baptism or falling of the Holy Spirit upon them (verse 5).

And the baptism was coming forth to enable these disciples to carry out God's plan.

> *"...but you shall receive power when the Holy Spirit has come upon you; and you shall be My witnesses both in Jerusalem, and in all Judea and Samaria, and even to the remotest part of the earth," Acts 1:8*

We who are present-day disciples are still recipients of that remarkable out-pouring of Holy Spirit power. The heavens will open and His Spirit can descend on us. It is high honor to be able to say, "The Spirit of the Lord us upon me." as we join our ancestors in faith to finish His work.

Second, in enjoying our ministries, we must agree about the Lord of the Spirit. In announcing His ministry, Jesus could declare He was Lord. We cannot—because we are not. There in only one Lord. Yet, while giving Jesus His proper place of exaltation, we can humbly understand we are His earthly representatives or agents. We are His human leaders or lords. We are those anointed to be in charge of certain things or to exercise divine authority in specific areas on earth.

Third, we will enjoy our ministries if we recognize proper boundaries. Though Jesus is Lord of all, our ministries have parameters. There are areas we are anointed to serve in and those we are not. Some have been given one talent, some ten and some even more. Yet no man operates in the multitudes of ways that Jesus did.

Happily, in yielding to His wise restriction, we learn that the Holy Spirit is a God of great diversity, inventiveness and originality. If truly in His Spirit, we will never be bored doing what He asks us to do. With His Spirit upon us, there are any number of venues, approaches, ways and means of innovatively doing the work.

For instance, if our general assignment is to preach the gospel, He may specifically direct us to do so by speaking or teaching, by composing, singing, or playing music, by presenting dance or drama, by making banners, by involvement in TV, radio, or tape ministries, by creating educational tools, holding seminars or workshops or by writing books. In and from the anointed expression of the word of God should flow the manifestation of the power of God.

Fourth, we will enjoy our ministries if we are definite about them. The clarity of the simple statement of truth, *"God has sent me to..."*, goes a long way to eliminate confusion, the disappointment of the expectation of a different type of ministry, or the attempts of unscrupulous men to manipulate us into doing what they want done. Or, from the receiver's point of view, it gives those we are sent to minister among a chance to discern if what we say is true and decide whether or not they want to yield to the anointing as long as the Spirit is on us.

Fifth, we will enjoy our ministry as Jesus makes it known. God raises up those He chooses to (Psalm 75:7). To enable them to do specific jobs, He gives them specific gifts. These gifts prepare their way (Proverbs 18:16). As the word went forth about Jesus before the onset of His public ministry (Luke 4:14), so knowledge of our special blessings will become known. Then, maybe or maybe not in as public a way as Jesus, in a time, way, and place of divine choosing, God will make it known that His Spirit is on us because He has anointed us to do certain things.

When Jesus was finished speaking, there were two reactions. The first was His own: "*He closed the book, and gave it back to the attendant, and sat down*". The second is that of the people: "*and the eyes of all in the synagogue were fixed upon Him*" (Luke 4:20).

When Jesus ended His announcement, He didn't continue on, He didn't embellish, He didn't discuss, and He didn't defend His words. He just sat down.

When Jesus ended His announcement, His listeners didn't' deny, they didn't protest, they didn't mock, and they didn't reject. Rather, they fixed their eyes on Him (NASB), fastened their eyes on Him (KJ), or gazed attentively at Him (AMP). Though trouble was soon coming, at that moment everyone was totally focused on Jesus, seeing Him, internalizing His words, wrapped in His presence. What better way to prosper in our ministries than to remain totally focused on Him?

Blessed is he who comes in the name of the LORD... Matthew 21:9

Chapter 16

The Spirit of the Lord

"TRUST IN THE LORD WITH ALL YOUR HEART, AND DO NOT LEAN ON YOUR OWN UNDER- STANDING. IN ALL YOUR WAYS ACKNOWL- EDGE HIM, AND HE WILL MAKE YOUR PATHS STRAIGHT." Proverbs 3:5,6

We cannot afford to misunderstand or underestimate the value of the Spirit of the Lord in our lives. We quench this Spirit at our own peril.

It is only by the Spirit of the Lord that we can understand what God wants done. It is only by the Spirit of the Lord that we are able to do it.

For the chosen of God, His Holy Spirit is an indispensable gift. He is the ultimate necessity and blessing for success in life and ministry. Though this lesson was once lost upon Israel, we must pray it has a better reception in the church.

Concerning Israel, long years ago God carried the Hebrew children out of Egypt on eagles' wings. Once in the desert, they were met with a series of challenges, each meant, in its outcome, to prove the love and provision of God. After building the tabernacle, establishing the priesthood and receiv- ing the Law (and laws), the Israelites had set forth from Sinai and drew near the Promised Land. God's children were on the verge of realizing His prom- ises, of gaining their inheritance, and of entering their rest.

By direct command of the Lord, twelve men were sent to spy out the land. Returning after forty days, the spies gave a glowing report about the fruitfulness of the land. But then, in spite of knowing it was God's intent that Israel should enter and occupy Canaan, ten of the twelve introduced rebellion.

Giving a bad report concerning the people of the land, they said:

> *"We are not able to go up against the people, for they are too strong for us." So they gave out to the sons of Israel a bad report of the land which they had spied out, saying, "The land through which we have gone, in spying it out, is a land that devours its inhabitants; and all the people whom we saw in it are men of great size. There also we saw the Nephilim (the sons of Anak are part of the Nephilim); and we became like grasshoppers in our own sight, and so we were in their sight." Numbers 13:31-33*

Yet two other spies, Caleb and then Joshua with him, saw things differently. Though they too had seen the physical problems with their physical eyes, they had also seen with their spiritual eyes. They had seen through God's eyes. Their response was entirely different.

> *And Joshua the son of Nun and Caleb the son of Jephunneh, of those who had spied out the land, tore their clothes; and they spoke to all the congregation of the sons of Israel, saying, "The land which we passed through to spy out is an exceedingly good land. If the LORD is pleased with us, then He will bring us into this land, and give it to us—a land which flows with milk and honey. Only do not rebel against the LORD; and do not fear the people of the land, for they shall be our prey. Their protection has been removed from them, and the LORD is with us; do not fear them." Numbers 14:6-9*

Sadly, they were ignored. Refusing to honor God's purpose in calling them as a separate, holy people, refusing to accept His chosen inheritance for them, refusing to believe His word, the majority ruled. The people did exactly as they had been cautioned not to do. They feared the people and rebelled against God.

Though pardoned for their sin by, *"The Lord slow to anger and abundant in loving kindness, forgiving iniquity and transgression;..."* (Numbers 14:18), the Israelites were yet punished for their disobedience. For forty years, everyone had to march through the desert until, *"your corpses shall fall in this wilderness, even all your numbered men, according to your complete number from twenty years old and upward, who have grumbled against me"* (verse 29). The wages of sin even then was death.

As the Spirit of the Lord led Israel to Canaan, so today He has led the church to its present position. God has made the church promises and we are quickly coming to the time of seeing them fulfilled. If the Lord has sent forth a few, His prophets, to see ahead, to foresee, to gain an initial perspective, it is because in spite of obvious obstacles and hindrances, He wants a good report. Though enemies abound and are strong and fortified, though foes persist and are large and numerous, the Lord will prevail. The church is able to conquer them by the power of the Spirit because *"their protection has been removed from them, and the Lord is with us;"* (Numbers 14:9).

When faced with the decision of moving into her promises and taking her land, the church must choose to obey the Spirit of the Lord. If we do not, we, like Israel, have rebelled against God. We have spurned the security of His presence and the truth of His promise. We have rejected the power of His Spirit and aborted His purposes.

As these lessons apply to the church as a whole, so they are warnings to each saint, too. Since the church is made up of the sum of all individual saints, what each does or does not do effects the health, power, and future of all.

When we are reborn spiritually, it is God's Holy Spirit who both indwells us and rests on us. It is this Spirit, the Spirit of the Lord, who is to communicate with our renewed human spirit to direct, test, guide, inform, teach, reveal to and lead us.

It is not uncommon that when each of us is reborn, we enter into a disciplinary process of learning and growing. Our intent is to follow Jesus, be like He was, do as He did, and in every way be obedient. But so often we get our eyes off Jesus and begin to focus on what we hope is the fruit of this effort—our miracle moment where we are healed or finances are secured or the ministry we've longed for seems to come together. What we may not realize is that life is a series of tests and our responses to seemingly insignificant choices determine whether or not there will ever be a "big" moment.

By His Spirit, (pillar and cloud), God led Israel; in like manner, by the Spirit of the Lord, He wants us to be led. By His Spirit, God tested Israel; in like manner, by the Spirit of the Lord, so He challenges us. By His Spirit, God led Israel to the land He had promised them; in like manner, by the Spirit of the Lord He leads us to our inheritance. And like Israel, we are given a choice: react in fear, revert to flesh, refuse to cooperate, and rebel against God or overcome the fear of man, stay in and with His Sprit, move forward and obey.

When we are secure in the fact that the Lord is with us and the Spirit is enabling us, our obedience brings those great times of blessings. When we are insecure in our relationship with God and unable to trust Him, our shrinking back brings judgment. Rebellion still comes at a high price.

But that is not the end of the story. After Israel's refusal to do as He commanded them to do and their disobedience in failing to take the land, there was more trouble. His children had sinned, God had spoken, God had judged, and God had pronounced what would happen next. Because of their rebellion, a successful military campaign was now to be a prolonged death trek.

The sons of Israel would not accept this. Perhaps hoping to remove the horrible judgment against them, they now determined to sin again by doing what they had just refused to do.

> *In the morning, however, they rose up early and went up to the ridge of the hill country, saying, "Here we are; we have indeed sinned, but we will go up to the place which the LORD has promised." Numbers 14:40*

Moses warned that the planned attack would fail.

> *"Why then are you transgressing the commandment of the LORD, when it will not succeed?" (verse 41)*

And he clearly stated why the outcome would be so disastrous.

> *"Do not go up lest you be struck down before your enemies, for the LORD is not among you." (verse 42)*

Ignoring him, proceeding without the ark of the Presence or Moses himself, the Israelites went up to the hill country. There just as prophesied, the Amalekites and Canaanites, *came down and struck them and beat them down...* (verse 45). Routed and defeated, Israel had again learned a hard lesson. Refusal to act when the Spirit of the Lord was with them was rebellion; acting when He was not with them was presumption.

When the Spirit of the Lord led Israel, it was expected Israel would follow. But when the Spirit of the Lord was not present, Israel should not have acted. Surely the church must learn the same lesson. Surely it must agree to act appropriately: where it is led, it must follow; where it is not led, it must not go.

As God has asked the church to move into certain places, so there are those that He has not. He has allowed some, His prophets, to voice His objections and declare the results of acting in presumption. Where He is with the church, there is victory; where He is not, there is death.

Presumption can rear its ugly head corporately in at least two obvious ways. First, following tradition for the sake of tradition, acting according to custom, convention, habit, routine, or taking it for granted that the Lord is honoring old rites and rituals could very well be presumption. Before asking saints to engage in certain activities, the church must always ask, "Is God in this or not?" If He is not, leading members in old, familiar religious practices, or allowing them to become involved in them is presumption.

Second, plunging into new fields of activity or diverting from a holy path without God's command or direction to do so is presumption. It is assuming to know the will of God without asking for it. The church, its denominations, its leaders, its local branches must seek the will of God through the Spirit of God and refrain from doing what He has not ordained. To fail to do so is to bring death upon itself.

As presumption affects the church as a whole, so it affects each saint. None of us has been given the authority to command our own lives—or anyone else's. Just as in the world there were some things that were not right for us or we were not asked to do, so in the church, each of us will be tempted to do things that are not right for us or which God has not asked us to do. Each of us at some time will long to fulfill the desires of our own heart, not His for us. At some point in our journey with Him, we will refuse God's will in order to engage in self selected (or man commissioned) activity. Even if we are good at that we've chosen to do, and even if it seems that He is honoring it, He will ultimately let us exhaust ourselves by doing it until we acknowledge it as presumption.

Just as deadly as planned presumption is spontaneous presumption. Surely there are times each Christian is asked to decide or move quickly on an issue and the result is not presumption. But all too often moving on unholy impulse, following whim, shooting from the hip, responding impetuously, or acting hastily from self desire and self confidence is. The difference between what is holy or what is human is where the motive for the action comes from: God or man?

Further, at some point, even if we have rebelled against God, have repented, and are now earnestly ready to serve Him, we cannot just proceed. We cannot assume that yesterday's order is today's command. Like Israel, we cannot make up for one sin by committing another. We are not authorized to do anything without hearing from or being directed by the Lord. If we aren't sure of His word to us or don't have His command for us, we must seek Him for it, search the scriptures, wait and pray. Then, only when we know, we can do as He has said.

We cannot presume to know God's plan for us. We cannot, either corporately or individually, make our own favorable decisions or act out our own fantasies and then say God ordained it. Moreover, when involved in ministry, we cannot ever self determine the purpose of the anointing of God on us or minister to others out of our own mind or heart. It would be impossible to calculate the offense to God or the damage to our victims this has caused.

We must constantly, consistently, always, ever seek God, search for His heart, wait to hear His voice that we may do or not do as He desires. To avoid rebellion, we must believe that we are "*strong in the Lord*" and our obedience is "*in the strength of* **His** *might*" (Ephesians 6:10). To not be found in presumption, we must understand that though positionally all things are under man's feet, man is only charged to rule over the works of His hands. (Psalm 8:6)—or do only those specific things God gives us to do.

If ever any two biblical accounts of sin and its fruit speak to today's church, these of rebellion and presumption do. God has in past days visited His church with times of revival or renewal, seasons when His Spirit has wonderfully invaded, overwhelmed, and rested upon His loved ones in a mantle of blessing and power. For those whose hunger for God has led to research of such happenings, the names of Azuza Street, Kentucky, Wales, and the healing ministries of the mid-twentieth century set hearts racing.

But all of these visitations of the presence and power of God through His Spirit, while blessings in themselves, have only served to set the stage for the final move of God in life as we know it now. While these revivals have been a blessing of obedience, when rebellion and/or presumption raised up, they failed or died out altogether. When He again presents Himself in power, these sins must not once again reject Him.

Jesus the Lord did so much while He was here on earth. Jesus, the living, ascended, and glorified Lord will do so much more before He returns, either in sovereign acts or by the power of His Spirit through men. Heaven will soon open and His Spirit will descend on the true body of Christ, superimposing Himself on it, pressing on it, imprinting Jesus on it, and resting on it. This Holy Spirit will enable the church to bring in the final harvest through anointed preaching of the word and manifestations of divine power.

The Lord who told Moses that "...*as I live all the earth will be filled with the glory of the LORD*" (Numbers 14:21), is about to fulfill His promise. The same Spirit that raised Jesus from the dead will quicken His body. He will pour over His people. Whole nations will fall before His wave of power. Whole denominations will renounce any unbiblical creeds and social heresies and yield to His sovereignty. Any gates not lifted up will be crushed and then brushed aside that the King of glory may come in!

Who is this King of glory? He is the LORD (Psalm 24:8)! He is the LORD strong and mighty! He is the LORD mighty in battle! He is the LORD of hosts!

And it is His Spirit, the Spirit of this mighty Lord, who will precede the Lord, prepare His way in power, and then present the Lord.

While waiting and preparing for that day, it is more important than ever that each saint repent of rebellion and presumption and yield to the Spirit of the Lord.

For some it may be easier to submit to God's way (the Spirit upon me) to do His will (because He anointed me to…) if we know why He is asking this of us. Though this is an inexhaustible subject worthy of intensive study, some of His reasons may be:

1. When we were unbelievers in the world of sin we were under the horrible tyranny and cruelty of the prince of the world, Satan. Then when we responded to the salvation message, repented, were forgiven of our sins and entered into right relationship with God, we took over the reins of government and assumed management of our lives; now we were led by the prince of self. We ruled our lives by flesh, whim, thought, emotion, or self will. If we are honest about this, we can only say that satanic rule was horrific or we wouldn't have wanted to escape it and that self rule was a failure which left us exhausted and unfulfilled. The Lord is presenting us with a better alternative: His Lordship. He wants to oversee or govern our lives. Rather than continuing to halt between two counterfeit authorities or to presumptuously assume He is our Lord, He is asking us to choose Him as Lord. He is willing, even anxious, to anoint us with His Spirit, commission us, present us with our tasks, and present us to others if we decide for, select, pick, prefer above all others, and embrace Him as Lord. He is Lord and we need His Spirit.

2. God is the only One with the plan. There is nothing we can do to change it. Neither can we substitute our own for it. Surely we cannot improve it. Since it's His plan, He's in charge of it. To fulfill our part in it, we need Him. He is Lord and we need His Spirit.

3. Although the Lord's plan doesn't change, our part in it occasionally does. What God anoints in one season of our lives may be superseded by a different anointing, gift mix, or enablement in another season. In doing this, He is not so much removing an empowerment as much as He is de-emphasizing one in favor of another. To receive His new or additional blessings, it is necessary to relinquish or lay aside the others either temporarily or perma-

nently as He chooses. If we receive a new anointing, we will enjoy new levels of power or areas of authority. If we refuse a new anointing we are idolizing the past, have walked out of His will, and reassumed self rule. Years later, we may yet be found going through the same old motions and wondering at the lack of results. Going through any such change can be smooth or it can be brutal. In either case, we need to stay close to God. He is Lord, and we need His Spirit.

4. God has made each of us a part of His body whose Head is Jesus. We each must do what we are commissioned to do or the body will not, indeed cannot, function effectively. If we don't do as we are asked to do or serve where we are asked to serve by the Head, we compromise the good of the whole church. He is Lord and we need His Spirit.

5. God wants us in close relationship and absolute dependence on Him. We can only find out what He wants done and how He wants it done by prayer, worship, and communication with Him, We can only share the excitement of our growth and victories by communing with Him. We can only acknowledge our defeats and seek wisdom by communing with Him. In building relationship with us, He has involved us in communicating with Him through His Spirit. Our hearts are thrilled to know that He loves us so much that He has built into our ministries the most important reason to continue to go back to our Source: His love for us. He is Lord and we need His Spirit.

The Spirit of the Lord GOD is upon me because the LORD has anointed me to.... Isaiah 61:1

Chapter 17

The Lord is the Spirit

O LORD, surely I am Thy servant, I am Thy servant, the son of Thy handmaid, Thou hast loosed my bonds. Psalm 116:16

There is one God. This singular, unique God is triune in nature. He is Father and so leads, guides, secures, protects, and provides for; He is Son, executor of holy, divine will; He is Holy Spirit, the power of the work.

In what is known as the high priestly prayer, or the words He spoke to His disciples just before His death, Jesus described the unity of the relationship of Father and Son.

> *And I am no more in the world; and yet they themselves are in the world, and I come to Thee, Holy Father, keep them in Thy name, the name which Thou hast given Me, that they may be one, even as We are. John 17:11*

In another place, scripture reveals the relationship between Son and Spirit: "*The Lord is the Spirit*" (2 Corinthians 3:17). The two are so intertwined, so together, so unified, so in focus regarding goals, ways and works as to be One.

We know the Lord is God (Psalm 100:3). And, that the Lord is the Son or Jesus has been documented in earlier portions of this book. Now, we must accept the biblical pronouncement that the Lord is also the Spirit. Keeping the unity of the triune God, Father, Son, and Spirit are Lord.

While the previous chapter about the Spirit of the Lord may seem cautionary in nature, there is a flip side. Though the Spirit of the Lord warns of sin and admonishes and counsels the saints of God or the church not to indulge in rebellion or presumption, it is the also Lord who is the Spirit who brings personal freedom and transformation.

First, in the work of the Lord who is the Spirit concerning our liberty, we all want to be free. Yet, never has any of us been truly free. Before our rebirth, we were anything but free; we were chained, bound, tied and imprisoned in the evils of Satan, sin, and the world. When the gospel message taught us this wasn't liberty and the Lord moved in our hearts to cause us to respond to His truth, we repented, confessed our sins, were forgiven of them through the shed blood of Jesus Christ and were translated into relationship with our Father, holiness, and the kingdom of God.

Sadly, in the immaturity our new found independence from evil, many of us began to plan and live lives of carnal, human pleasure where self determination ruled. We called our own shots, kept our own schedules, and did what was right in our own eyes. Then as a result of God's graciousness and patience, reality set in. This wasn't freedom either. We were in fact in bondage to flesh and self. Knowing this wasn't where we wanted to live and die, the only option left was to release ourselves into the care of God. To a small, genuinely puzzled few, the question, "Can serving yet another Master be called freedom?" needs to be answered.

The dealings of God with the Israelites help us to understand. The Hebrews were a people who struggled with two veils. One was a physical, material veil worn by Moses because of men's fears. The other, a spiritual evil covering the minds of the people, was brought on by rebellion and obstinacy. Both veils hid God from men, leaving them anything but free. Because of the veil of fear, they were not free to enjoy personal relationship with God; because of the veil of blinded minds, they were not free in the truth.

Concerning the physical veil, thousands of years ago two or three million Hebrews were emancipated from Egypt, In the third month after their Exodus, they came to the foot of Mt. Sinai. There Moses *"went up to God and the LORD called to Him from the mountain."* (Exodus 19:3). In this meeting, God gave Moses the Ten Commandments, various ordinances and rules for community living, and His requirements regarding His feasts. Moses then went down the mountain to establish covenant between God and the Israelites (Exodus 19:25).

Recalled to the presence of God, Moses ascended the mountain a second time. In this meeting, God gave Moses the plan for the tabernacle, the priests, and the sacrifices or the means by which the accepted covenant would be kept and worship offered. Then, angry at a people who had already corrupted themselves through rebellion and idolatry, God sent Moses down the mountain to discipline.

Shattering the tablets of stone which had been inscribed with the Law and scattering the gold dust from the idol which the rebellious people had made, it was apparent to all that while there had been no freedom in sin in Egypt, there was no freedom in sin in the desert either.

Again Moses ascended Mt. Sinai, this time to ask for forgiveness for the sins of the people (Exodus 32:31). Later, in the midst of trying to establish God's authority over the people, the Word notes a wonderful thing.

> *Now Moses used to take the tent and pitch it outside the camp, a good distance from the camp, and he called it the tent of meeting. And it came about, that everyone who sought the LORD would go out to the tent of meeting which was outside the camp. And it came about, whenever Moses entered the tent, the pillar of cloud would descend and stand*

at the entrance of the tent; and the LORD would speak with Moses.
Thus the LORD used to speak to Moses face to face, just as a man speaks
to his friend. Exodus 33: 7,9,11

It was in this face-to-face relationship that Moses asked the Lord to, "...*let me know Your ways, that I may know Thee...*" (verse 13). Here he pressed until the LORD agreed to continue to go with Israel on their journey (verse 17). And here, in intimate communion, Moses dared to ask for a blessing. In a request that should echo the longing of our own hearts, he said to the LORD, "*I pray Thee, show me Thy glory!*" (verse18).

At first Moses' desire was refused. For safety's sake, God said no. But then, almost as if pleased with a child or as if He couldn't help Himself for the joy of it, God made a way. He hid Moses in the cleft of a rock, shielded him from life threatening outpourings of His glory but let him see His back.

This time when Moses descended the mountain, it was neither to cut covenant nor to discipline. Instead it was to reveal the spiritual authority given to His servant and to manifest the presence of God through His servant. When Moses came down Mt. Sinai, he was so wrapped in God's holiness, so enraptured with His Person, so engulfed in His Being that his face shone. The presence of God so covered Moses with holy radiance that the LORD could visibly be seen on him (Exodus 34: 29).

The reaction to this outpouring of glory was fear (verse 30). Because the sons of Israel were afraid to come near him, after speaking with the rulers of the people, Moses, "*put a veil on his face*". (verse 33). This was not a one-time experience. Veiling the presence of God became the norm in his life (verse 34,35).

Moses had met the Light, and His glory had so infused and infilled Moses that it was visibly shining through him. He had met God with unveiled face and communed with Him. The people however had no such blessing. Their fear so paralyzed them that they didn't even want to look at the splendor of the presence of their God. Therefore, Moses who saw the glory wore the veil; the others who didn't see were blinded. They were not free in their fear to come closer to God or enter personal relationship with Him.

The spiritual veil over Israel was an even deeper prison. Moses' veil blocked their eyes; the next veil blocked their minds and hearts.

When the Hebrews entered Canaan, they were to take the land and deal with the inhabitants. As years passed, they saw many things, but seldom the presence of God. When Jesus came, they were unable to see that the physical son of Joseph and Mary was the holy Son of God. They had no insight that His works evidenced the kingdom of God among them. They were blind to the fact that the anointing on Him made Him the Christ, the Messiah.

Further, during these centuries of blindness, they added to God's commandments, binding men to oral law and the traditions of men. The Jewish mind was so steeped in scripture, so learned in law, so encompassed with the past, so controlled by ritual that it became blind to the truth. With a veil blinding their minds, they were unable to truly think, reason, or know. With a veil over their emotions, they were unable to feel. With a veil covering their wills, they were unable to make wise decisions. Not having been spiritually reborn, this was a people walking in the strength of soul and body. And with the functions of their mind compromised and impaired, this was a people living in flesh. They were not free to see God; they were not free to find Him in their scripture.

Rather than condemning the Israelites too harshly for their physical and spiritual shortcomings, we should realize that some of us have the same problem. Because we didn't want to see, we can't see. Because we refused to see, we are blind. We look for Jesus and can't find Him; we read the Bible and its stories are nice but bring no life. In truth, we have lost our liberty. We are bound and a veil blocks us both from the presence of God and from the knowledge of God.

But, where the Lord is the Spirit, both problems are resolved.

> *...but whenever a man turns to the Lord, the veil is taken away. Now the Lord is the Spirit; and where the Spirit of the Lord is, there is liberty.* 2 Corinthians 3:16,17

When Jesus hung on the cross and the veil of His flesh was torn (Hebrews 10:20), provision was made that we may see. His sacrifice is our means of sight and vision. It removed our blindness. We who have accepted His sacrifice can now, like Moses, approach Jesus, enter His presence through the Open Veil and commune with Him face to face. In the Holy of Holies, in His awesome presence, we can see Him as He is. Soulish fear and dread yield to holy fear and reverence. And at the same time that the restriction of our face-to-face intimacy with God is done away with, the dark, confusing, obstructing veil is removed from our minds so we can read and understand scripture in spirit. Suddenly our Bibles are not just words but holy words inspired by the Holy Spirit. And reading them, rereading them, meditating on them, praying about them, communing with God concerning them, and obeying them brings direction (truth to live by) and life. This is true freedom.

Where the Lord is the Spirit, we are free to choose God. We have the freedom to refuse evil or human rule and choose God's holy government over us. Where the Lord is the Spirit, we see God and know Him. And we choose, by a deliberate act of will, to obey Him. This is not bondage. The truth has set us free.

In addition to liberty, the second great blessing of the Lord who is the Spirit is transformation. Following salvation, it is the Spirit's job to change us.

> *But we all, with unveiled face beholding as in a mirror the glory of the Lord, are being transformed into the same image from glory to glory, just as from the Lord, the Spirit.* 2 Corinthians 3:18

From the time of our physical birth to the moment of our spiritual rebirth, all of us lived in the world. There, under its master, Satan, we could not help but be affected by and even be a part of its ways, values, culture, social agenda, tolerance and permissiveness toward sin,... and the practice of evil. Its ways were our ways. By no stretch of the imagination could any of this be called Christlike. Thankfully, wonderfully, by the blessing of the Lord who is the Spirit, none of us has to remain in that condition. Each of us can be transformed into the image of God's Son who Himself is the exact image or representation of God (Hebrews 1:3).

Funk and Wagnall's Dictionary defines transformation as to give a different form to, to change the character of, to alter the nature of, to convert, or to be fashioned anew. Vine's Expository Dictionary of Biblical Words agrees with this, adding the idea of undergoing a complete inward change which is seen in outward character and conduct.

Three things are important to understand about this transformation. First, it is not something we do to or for ourselves. It is a blessing given us, as we cooperate with the power of the Spirit upon and within us. The command to be transformed (Romans 12:2) and the statement that we are being changed (2 Corinthians 3:18) both indicate activity on our behalf or something being done for us. We in our freedom must choose to allow the work to be done and participate with God in it, but it is the Lord who is the Spirit who does the transforming.

Second, transformation is not a one-time event. When released from the kingdom of darkness and admitted to the kingdom of God, we are positionally saved and sanctified. But the transformation of nature, alteration of character, conversion of values and priorities, and our becoming new creations is a process. We move from place to place, glory to glory, under the watchful, careful guidance of God's Spirit.

Third, there is a specific goal in mind for such a protracted metamorphosis. The Spirit molds, squeezes, stretches, shapes, and alters us so that we become like Christ. When the veils are removed from eyes and mind, when we can physically and spiritually see, the Spirit transforms us so that in looking upon ourselves we no longer see our own image but that of Christ in us. As we behold Him, we are inwardly changed to be like Him. Then all we say and do outwardly is an expression of Him to the world.

(Please understand that in all of this transformation, while we grow like the Lord, we never become the Lord. We become like He is or after the manner of Christ, but we never reach His stature. We resemble, are similar to, have the nature of, and conform to the image of Jesus, but we are not Jesus. We are not the Lord.)

We with unveiled face look in a mirror, see Jesus, and are changed into His image, becoming like Him. We are not to be like Satan who said, *"I will ascend to heaven; I will raise my throne above the stars of God; I will sit on the mount of the assembly in the recesses of the north; I will ascend above the heights of the clouds; I will make myself like the Most High"* (Isaiah 14:13,14). What he really meant was, "I want equality with God. In fact, I want to be higher than God."

Nor are we to be like man who wants supremacy and sovereignty to carnally rule over the affairs of men.

Our being like God is not to rise to take His place. It is not to compete with Him for first place. He is the only begotten Son while we are adopted into His family; though we are kings, He is the King; though we are lords, He is Lord; though we are priests, He is High Priest. He was the sinless Sacrifice and we are not. Because of our sin, He was the only One worthy to approach the Father and provide forgiveness; we are the recipients of the manifold blessings that are the fruit of His love. We must always desire to become like Him but never, never should we challenge or presume to become Him.

Most of us are honest enough to admit---if only in private moments---that there are things about ourselves we don't like and wish we could change.

Many of us are also honest enough to admit we have tried to change and failed. Now we understand the reason of our failure. The task was not our job. We were trying to do the work of the Holy Spirit for Him. Part of our transformation is realizing that we cannot change ourselves. He alone is Lord. He alone is responsible to change us. In our metamorphosis, sovereign God initiates, we cooperate, but it is the Spirit who transforms.

When we die, are buried, and resurrected to new life, we are not raised to continue life as it was. We are raised under the Lordship of Christ. He has become our Ruler, Leader, Governor. We are to grow to resemble Him in character and nature.

A portion of the anointing on Him is now on us. That anointing is to be used only to do as He would do. We must be changed into His image to have the inner strength to be as He is and the outward power to do as He does. All of this a part of the transformation process of the Lord who is the Spirit.

As members of the kingdom of God, the Lord helps us to lay aside our unholy judgments, thoughts, and attitudes and introduces us to the mind of Christ. He helps us quell our unholy feelings and sinful attempts to express God-given emotions and gives us the passions of Christ. He gives us the desires of our hearts, His desires for us, so we will do as He wants done.

As He transforms our inner man, we find we are outwardly different, too. Our obedience to His calling on our lives reflects the alterations He has wrought in our nature and character, changes which can be seen in our behavior. For instance, if we are really being transformed, should He ask us to be pastors, because we know He is chief Shepherd and therefore Lord over any and every pastorate, our ministry to His sheep will reflect His image. We will be found nurturing, healing, caring for, feeding, guiding, and maturing the flock just as Jesus did.

Similarly, if we are called to preach, teach, heal, deliver, disciple, or serve in any outward way, we can only do so through the transforming power of the Spirit of God in us and through us. It is only by His Spirit in us that we are made whole and only by His Spirit upon and through us that others are made whole.

The Scripture about transformation is found in the last verse of 2 Corinthians 3, a chapter concerned with ministers. Paul compares Christians to letters of Christ, written by the Spirit of the living God and declared us adequate as ministers or servants of the New Covenant **by the Holy Spirit**. He asks us to ponder how the ministry of the letter of the law which brought condemnation and death but yet evidenced enough of the glory of God to require Moses to cover his face compares with the ministry of the Spirit who brings life and pours forth the glory of God in a way that we may see, we may know, and we may be changed to become a part of.

New Covenant ministers must be free of rather than resemble Satan. New Covenant ministers must be free of rather than adapted and obedient to habitual sin. New Covenant ministers must be free of rather than conformed to the world in social and cultural values. New Covenant ministers must be free of rather than reconciled to self with its impure thoughts, unholy expressions of holy emotions, and self will. New Covenant ministers must be free of acquiescence to demands, commands, and traditions of men. To be in this place of freedom, they must be transformed into the image of Jesus Christ who is Victor and Lord over them all.

A New Covenant minister is one who, like Moses, asks to see the glory of God. He is one who positions himself to see. She is one who casts off all self cares and fears in her desire to see. And the radiance and glory of seeing infuses each with the light of Christ.

A New Covenant minister is one who accepts the word as absolute truth and by it strips off all faulty theology, doctrinal error, and denominational disagreement and simply sees Jesus.

A New Covenant minister forsakes all confidence in self and yields to the Spirit of the Lord. He entrusts his whole being into His keeping. She is so smitten with, captivated by, and astonished by the Lord who is the Spirit that she surrenders all to Him. Each, in surrendering self, gives Him permission to transform him from glory to glory into His own image.

The Lord who is the Spirit brings us into liberty. We are free to know Him. The Lord who is the Spirit transforms us. In knowing Him, we are free to become like Him. Our freedom is that we can choose to serve and worship the Lord who taught and transformed us.

What shall I render to the LORD for all His benefits toward me? I shall lift up the cup of salvation, and call upon the name of the LORD.   Psalm 116:12,13

Chapter 18

WHAT IS THE OPEN HEAVEN?

After these things I looked, and behold, a door standing open in heaven.....Revelation 4:1

Scripture has revealed that a Man, Jesus, the Son of God, went to the Jordan River and was baptized to fulfill all righteousness (Matthew 3:15). His baptism in water was followed by His baptism or immersion into the Spirit of God. When He arose from the river, the Holy Spirit in the form of a dove descended from heaven and came upon Him (Matthew 3:16). That same experience is available to us.

After we have personally appropriated Jesus' provision of salvation and been reborn spiritually, we can receive His provision of strength and ability and be enabled spiritually. Our deadened spirits that He quickened to new life are authorized or commissioned to do His works in power.

After Passover, the sons of Israel celebrated the feast of Pentecost. To many in the Hebrew culture, the first was not considered over until the second had been completed. Just so, we as Christians can follow up our Passover experience, salvation, with a celebration of Pentecost or the Holy Spirit coming down upon us. Through what the Bible refers to as, "*baptized with the Holy Spirit.*" (Acts 1:5), the body of Christ and all of its members can receive the power to be His, *"witnesses in Jerusalem, and in all of Judea, and Samaria, and even to the remotest part of the earth."* (Acts 1:8). For us to do what He wants us to do, He must enable us, and His means of accomplishing this universally wide task is by His Holy Spirit on us and then through us.

Going past the Open Veil, we enter the Open Heaven. To walk here successfully, we must understand what the Open Heaven is. Perhaps the understanding of the Open Heaven will be clearer as we compare it with the Open Veil. While both are God initiated, they have different functions, focus and fruit. While both surely overlap and integrate, there are some discernible differences.

The Open Veil	The Open Heaven
our Passover	our Pentecost
Salvation	Sanctification
Savior	Lord
Holy Spirit in	Holy Spirit on
Fruit of the Spirit	Gifts of the Spirit
Being as He is	Doing as He does
Death, Burial, Resurrection	New life in Christ
Entering in	Walking it out
Relationship with	Sent out by
Hearing	Obeying

Further, we can clarify what The Open Heaven is by first declaring what it is not. The Open Heaven is

NOT self empowerment or using holy power for human reasons

NOT license to do what, when, where, and how we please

NOT accomplishing or even attempting to accomplish the desires of our own hearts, the demands on us by others (family, friends), fulfilling the will of God for the wrong reasons (financial gain, promotion, status).

The Open Heaven is submitting to the Lordship of Jesus Christ and doing what he wants done in His way by His strength.

- It is understanding the difference and division between the world and the Kingdom of God, and knowing that each saved saint has been brought out of one to enter the other.

- It is realizing that no saint can submit to the government of Satan any longer and so must reject his demonic rule and false authority and submit to the leadership of Jesus Christ.

- It is knowing that satanic means and human methods are not God's ways.

- It is severance of satanic rule, refusal of self rule, and acceptance of holy sovereignty.

- It is acknowledging there is one gospel, one Lord and one Spirit and knowing that any who proclaims another gospel which honors another lord who empowers by another spirit has missed the Open Heaven.

- It is agreeing that Jesus did the will of His Father and though He finished His own course, left much for the church to do. Faith without works is dead.

- It is knowing with certainty that without Jesus we can do NOTHING! It is stripping away all desire to do so, and in that helpless state surrendering to our Lord who can do everything and wants to do through us. As He was assigned general responsibilities and specific tasks to accomplish by the power of the Spirit, so He, our Lord, now assigns us tasks which He completes through us by that same Spirit.

The Open Heaven is acceptance of the Holy Spirit to both dwell in us and empower us.

- It is willingly approaching Jordan, the place of death.

- It is welcoming, receiving, accepting, and delighting in the Holy Spirit as He comes to rest on us.

- It is being anointed by the Holy Spirit to have the strength, ability, and power to do as He did.

- It is understanding that as Jesus' public ministry began after the Holy Spirit alighted on Him, rested on Him, and anointed Him, so too with us. Our more outward activities or our ministries are contingent upon the Holy Spirit coming down on us and resting or staying on us to work through us.

- It is to look forward to and yield to the Lord's choice of baptism. Whether the Holy Spirit comes to us in the form of a dove as He did with Jesus, whether He appears as tongues of fire as He did with those waiting for Him in Jerusalem, or whether He reveals Himself in an altogether new manifestation, we are to receive of His fullness.

- It is to understand that kingdom life is contingent upon relationship with Jesus Christ, the Lord, not with His power. Though He is revealed in life, it is the deeper revelation that He becomes our very life. It is coming to the ocean that is Christ and instead of staying on shore, it is plunging into His deeper depths and higher heights, glorying in the increased awareness of who He is.

- It is agreeing to bear fruit.

The Open Heaven is testing, not of power, but of character.

- To see if we will truly submit to the will of God.

- To see if we will follow holy command.

- To see if we will refuse to use holy power for unholy reasons.

- To see if we will reject personal comfort, glory, ambition and self aggrandizement and refuse to be like Simon the Sorcerer who wanted the Spirit to dazzle the people and draw attention to himself or to see if we will focus on humbly doing the will of the Father as directed by the Son by the power of their Spirit.

- In a specific reference to the power rather than the presence of the Spirit, it is to survive the sifting out process. God does not trust His power to those unwilling to honor it as holy both in source and in intent. He is not required to honor what He has not ordained; He will not empower what He has not commanded. Those refusing to yield to His authority are weeded out. While they may claim to be of God, go through motions that seem to honor His ways, their ministry is a counterfeit and a sham. At best they are serving self; at worst they are angels of light promoting Satan.

The Open Heaven is entry into God's will for our lives.

- It is hearing His call and entering in.

- As there are tests concerning empowerment, there are temptations concerning calling. The Open Heaven is to discern human (family, friend, minister, boss) demands on our lives and to reject all that do not agree with God's will for us.

- It is to honestly assess personal goals, dreams, plans and desires and to disencumber ourselves of those whose source is not God. It is giving up our own heart's desires and allowing God to impregnate us with the desire of His heart for us.

- The call is not just a job description. It also included attitudes (fearful, positive, angry), personal traits (dishonest, truthful, punctual), and the presence of strongholds (jealousy, control, idolatry) which, if they are unChristlike, must be dealt with before we bring them to the work. It is discerning any plans or hindrances Satan has for our lives concerning these things and rebuking them. It is identifying personal stumbling stones, repenting and confessing sin where necessary and doing all possible to separate from them.

- It is to understand God's true plan for us in every age and season and serve Him there.

- It is to see as much of the overall plan as He shows us, find our specific role, and then thank Him for all the preparation, both pleasant and not so pleasant, that has led us to be able to say, "Yes, Lord!

- It is waiting for the day, time, and way He will raise us up and allow our calling to be declared before those to whom He chooses to reveal it.

The Open Heaven Is Obedience.

- It is accomplishing God's will God's way. It is staying on His task for us. It is finishing His assignment for us.

- It is pressing in after being pressed on by His Holy Spirit.

- It is continuing the works of Jesus here on earth.

- It is doing as He commands, no more, no less, no rebellion, no presumption.

- It is understanding that Israel was severely disciplined even to the loss of a generation of life because they would not separate the sacred from the profane—or obey the will of God.

The Open Heaven Is Change.

- It is a change of perspective. We see Jesus and others see Jesus on us.

- It is a change of direction.

- It is a change in the usual ways of doing things.

- It is a change of heart.

- It is a change outwardly regarding life style, goals, and abilities.

- It is a change inwardly concerning character and nature.

The Open Heaven is God.

- Coming down in glory and power.

- It is His presence and power on earth.

- It is God rolling up His sleeves to finish the work.

- It is Jesus seeing a need, coming up behind us, reaching out to touch us, creating a connection or plugging us into His power and doing what needs to be done through us.

- It is seeing as He sees, hearing as He hears, saying what He says, doing as He does.

- It is His power upon those who recognize, accept, honor, and are submitted to both the Spirit of God and the God of the Spirit.

- It is the presence and power of God in us so we can represent Him to the world.

- It is the presence and power of God on us to fulfill the Great Commission.

- It is Christ in us, our hope of glory and the Spirit on us because He has anointed us.

"MAKE READY THE WAY OF THE LORD, MAKE HIS PATHS STRAIGHT." Luke 3:4

"BLESSED IS HE WHO COMES IN THE NAME OF THE LORD;" Matthew 21:9

"...Strengthen your hearts for the coming of the Lord is at hand." James 5:8

Afterword

Wonderfully, the Bible, history books, biographies, commentaries and sermons are filled with the names and stories of those who have called Jesus Lord. And yet, there is one who did not. There is one who would not, in time of crisis, acknowledge this fact or address Him as such. History has never stopped announcing or denouncing his treachery.

To recall, throughout His years of public ministry, Jesus lived a public life. He called a small troop of men around Himself and lived with them, walked with them, and talked with them. He shared good times and bad with them. Whether on a mountain, by a lake, or wandering a byway, each day He mentored, led, guided, and taught them.

Following word by power, Jesus proved He was Lord. He healed among them, raised the dead, showed astonishing authority over the forces of nature and performed miracles. In exhorting them to be as He was and do as He did, He changed an unruly mob of men, former fishermen and tax collectors, into followers. His disciplines then created disciples.

Without doubt, it can be said that He knew them well; and they, this privileged twelve, more than any others alive at that time knew Him intimately. In His leadership, He was patient, faithful, merciful, understanding, and good. He loved them. All of them. Even when He knew that one of them was nursing the seeds of bitterness, rebellion and disaster, He loved them.

As the days approached for what would be His final journey to the holy city, He became even more open, disclosing to them what was about to happen to Him. After His triumphal entry into Jerusalem, He taught in parables, rebuked religious leaders and warned of perilous times soon to come. One of His most poignant acts was to allow a woman to break open an expensive alabaster vial and pour its perfumed contents on His head (Matthew 26:7).

Instead of responding to her gesture of love with grace and honor, the disciples were indignant at what they judged as waste (verse 8). Jesus was aware that this woman knew something that His disciples did not. He knew she was prophetically grieving His death. To honor her act, He reproached His twelve by explaining.

> But Jesus, aware of this, said to them, "Why do you bother the woman? For she has done a good deed to Me. For the poor you have with you always; but you do not always have Me. For when she poured this perfume upon My body, she did it to prepare Me for burial. Truly I say to you, wherever this gospel is preached in the whole world, what this woman has done shall also be spoken of in memory of her." Matthew 26:10-13

But one of the twelve still seethed. As treasurer of the group (John 13:29), he knew the monetary cost of the vial with its perfume but not its value to the Lord. As thief (John 12:6), he probably wanted to pocket some of the money realized from its sale if it had remained unbroken. As rebel, the Lord's explanations were not accepted. Going far beyond indignation, his response was more lethal: betrayal unto death. He went to the chief priests and sold Jesus out (verse 14).

It was at the last meal, the celebration of Passover, that his treachery became apparent. Gathering the twelve, Jesus announced that one among them world betray Him (verse 21).

That pierced the hearts of eleven men. Deeply grieved, astonished, perhaps confused, "...*each one began to say to Him, 'Surely not I, **Lord**?'*" (verse 22) (emphasis mine)

.Each in his own way was saying that this betrayal was impossible. Each was eager to publicly and personally ascertain that this disclosure of treachery lay with someone else. Each was really saying, "O Lord Adonai, Lord Kurios, Lord Jesus, let it not be me! Please Lord, Leader, Master, know that it is not me!"

But there were twelve men gathered and twelve who heard Jesus' words. While eleven expressed shock at what they had heard and sought after and submitted their hearts to their Lord, there was a totally different reaction from the other man, Judas Iscariot.

His unique reaction was his refusal to acknowledge that Jesus was Lord.

After Jesus relieved the eleven of their anxiety by declaring their innocence, *"…that he who dipped his hand with Me in the bowl is the one who will betray Me"* (verse 23), Judas belatedly spoke up. Though seeming to echo the sentiment and concern of the other men, he significantly changed the title of the One he addressed. His own words convict him.

> *And Judas, who was betraying Him, answered and said, "Surely it is not I, **Rabbi**?" (verse 25) (emphasis mine)*

By calling Jesus Rabbi instead of Lord, he was denying His deity. In addressing Him as Rabbi instead of Lord, he was humanizing the divine One. Instead of as Sovereign of the heavens and earth, he was referring to Jesus as an honored and skilled teacher.

Perhaps because he could not or would not recognize Jesus as Lord or address Him as such, it made it easier for Judas to do what he was going to do. Perhaps because he lowered his estimation of Jesus from Lord of all to teacher of Scripture, He was easier to reject and betray. If that was Judas' thought, then he was not rejecting the Lord, but the man who made the mistake about the money and the vial. He was not betraying the Sovereign, but a teacher whose example of mercy and love was not acceptable to him.

Having already bargained with the chief priest and religious leaders, he doubled his treachery by guiding them to Jesus. Soon after supper, Judas led an armed multitude to Gethsemane and hunted Jesus down. As if in final insult, he greeted Him and once again addressed Him with the denigrating title: *"Hail, Rabbi!"* and kissed Him." (verse 49). Even at this last moment when he could have recognized Jesus as Lord, he chose not to—to his own destruction.

The lessons for all of us are profound. Surely there are times when we don't understand the thoughts and plans of the Lord or when His wisdom, mercy and compassion go beyond us. Just as surely, there are times we don't agree with what He is doing but in Christ find grace to submit to His right to rule. But never can there be a time that we demote Him to the status of man and betray Him to unbelievers—even if they are in the religious community—around us. If we do so, it will ultimately be to our own loss and ruin. We will discover to our sorrow that in betraying the Lord, we have really betrayed ourselves.

Judas was right in saying that Jesus was Teacher. But in this case, that title was inappropriate. The issue was obedience to the declared will of the Lord, not instruction.

The truth is that Jesus was Teacher and Lord (John 13:13). Eleven disciples acknowledged and related to Jesus in both His titles; one did not. Since Judas would not submit to the latter, he could only make reference to the former. And he died a horrible death estranged from the Lord he denied.

Therefore I make known to you, that no one speaking by the Spirit of God says, "Jesus is accursed"; and no one can say, "Jesus is Lord," except by the Holy Spirit. (1 Corinthians 12:3)

Jesus,

We pause now to honor You. You are the Lord. You are our Lord. You are the only Lord. Relationship with You, being in covenant with You, is our privilege and blessing. We exalt You. We call You Lord. You are Master, Leader, Ruler. You are Sovereign, the Lord of lords, Lord over all. Fill us with an overwhelming joy, delight and eagerness to submit to You as Lord. Let our voices sing, our hands clap, our feet dance as we celebrate You. Let all that is within us praise and worship You. Let the heavens and earth rise in unanimous acclamation:

Jesus Christ is Lord,
Jesus Christ is Lord,
Jesus Christ is Lord

because sovereign God made Him Lord.
Amen and amen.

www.ingramcontent.com/pod-product-compliance
Lightning Source LLC
Chambersburg PA
CBHW030006110426

42736CB00040BA/520